Live Your **YOU**logy

Six Secrets to

Discovering and Living

Your True Passion

Red Katz

David,
Thank you for your unselfish &
unconditional support, guidance & friendship
You are a huge blessing in my life.

In Gratitude,
Red

ISBN: 0989749509

ISBN 13: 9780989749503

Library of Congress Control Number: 2013913341

Red Inspires, New York, NY

"When it comes to delivering a message with impact, purpose and passion, Red Katz is the one to turn to. Through his humor, he can engage your audience to examine personal and professional challenges, and come out with hope towards the future. Live Your YOUlogy is the gateway to living your dream life. He walks his talk. Any opportunity to hear him speak or read his book is a gift."

– Alex Von Bidder, Managing Partner, The Four Seasons Restaurant

"In this rich little book - clearly a labor of love - Red Katz shares business and life success secrets that are sharp, well-written, and loaded with real-life lessons. Each chapter is a detailed snapshot of a successful habit, trait, or practice. Unlike most authors, who portray themselves as infallible heroes, Red portrays the real heart of our journey - the uncertainty, the fears, the doubts, the setbacks, the pivots and twists and turns. This is a book you'll want to come back to over and over again as your own business and personal adventures evolve and progress. Highly recommended for anyone who wants to start living larger, dreaming bigger, and achieving more."

– David Newman, Author of *Do It! Marketing*

"Refreshing. Honest. Inspiring. Live Your YOUlogy is a must-read for anyone who wants to live a happy, deeply satisfying life. Red tells it like it is, compelling you to not only want to know more about him and his experiences, but helping you learn more about yourself at the same time. No doubt that your life will be changed for the better once you let Red Katz into it. He is motivation at its finest."

– Christina DeBusk, Author of *The 15 Minute Total Life Makeover*

To Michaela, Ariel, Zoe, Phyl, Mom and Dad.
This book would not have been written
without each and every one of you in my life.
I am eternally blessed and grateful.
All my love.

I am just a simple man with a simple message. I'm not perfect. I don't know everything. I have made mistakes and will continue to make them. Thank you for picking up my book. I am honored that you value it enough to take the time to read it. My hope is that you'll incorporate what you learn from it into your life. My goal is to help the world become a better place for all, and my wish for you is that you live the passionate life you were meant to live.

Peace and Love,

Red

Contents

Preface

"We must believe that we are gifted for something
and that this thing, at whatever cost, must be attained."
Marie Curie (1867–1934), French Physicist, Chemist
and two-time Nobel Prize winner

What will people say about you after you're gone?
What have you done that people will remember you by?
Have you lived a life worth remembering?
Have you lived the life you were meant to live?
Is your life filled with passion and purpose?
Are you doing what you were meant to do in your life?
Are you living your life, or are you "dying" your life?

These are questions I ask myself daily and, in my humble opinion, contemplating these questions would help all of us live better, more fulfilling lives. This is a book that is going to help you find some of those answers.

First, however, here's a little bit about me and why I'm writing this book in the first place. As you know from the cover, my name is Red Katz and one of the reasons I was put on this earth is to inspire and motivate people.

I haven't always had inspirational and motivational things to say, trust me. Once upon a time, I was just a regular family man running my own business. I was also a happily married man and the father of three adorable kids, living my dream life on the Upper West Side of Manhattan.

Although I made my living as a businessman, I had also taken acting classes for years. I felt this inner urge to be on stage, to let all my emotions out, to perform. However, I grew tired of repeating the same tired lines from those "hacks" like, you know, Shakespeare and Eugene O'Neill. So I started writing my own monologues and, before I knew it, I had written an entire one-man show—a "dramedy" (heavy on the comedy, light on the drama)—appropriately named *A Day in the Life.*

Married, plus kids, plus adult responsibilities meant I couldn't really go through the regular channels hustling around Broadway to find a producer, so I decided to put on the show myself. I found an off-Broadway theater to rent, had a friend direct me and, for two glorious nights, *A Day in the Life* ran on, or at least close to, the big shows.

Then, life got in the way. *Big* time. You name it, I lived through it—divorce, bankruptcy, anxiety, depression, living in my brother's basement. You get the picture. It wasn't just a perfect storm of life events all conspiring to bring me down. This was a perfect tsunami that basically wiped clean the old slate of my life and brought me back to square one.

So there I sat, literally living underground like some kind of hobbit. As I began to drag myself out of a deep depression and started to recover from some of my financial mess, I began writing again. This time it was a new one-man play, a new way to vent my frustrations and find humor in the proceedings at the same time. I was able to write it easily enough, however I simply had no desire to make people laugh anymore—no energy for putting my show on *any* part of Broadway.

Producing *A Day in the Life* had been like a walk in the park and I loved it. However, this time around, every sentence was like pulling teeth without any laughing gas. I couldn't understand why the drama of my own life—always a popular topic in Red Land—wasn't drawing me in like it did the first time. I just wasn't feeling it. Although I got through the first draft, the thought of renting out a theater, finding a director and putting on my second show in front of people just left me feeling cold, blah, meh.

Fortunately, I belonged to a wonderful men's empowerment and support group that had been helping me through all of my life's challenges. (I still belong to that group and attend meetings to this day, which you'll hear more about later.) Hearing me complain about my stalled show, one of the group's members, my friend Mark, said to me, "Hey, Red, have you ever considered motivational speaking?"

I stood there, mouth open. Up to that moment, I had never even heard of a motivational speaker. I didn't know such people existed. But suddenly I knew that inspiring people was what I was meant to do. In fact, the more I thought about my friend's suggestion, the more my mind wouldn't let it go.

I realized why my new one-man show simply wasn't resonating with me, wasn't clicking like the first one did. Now that I'd seen the hard side of life and been through some rough times, I wanted to do more than just make people laugh. Perhaps motivational speaking would allow me to inspire them as well?

Well, that was years ago, and I've made good on my desire to "inspire." In fact, my life's mission is to create a loving and joyous world by accepting and empowering everyone. And every time I speak, tell my stories and share the tools that have helped me succeed, grow and prosper, someone inevitably approaches me and asks, "Have you ever written a book?"

For years I've promised them that I would have a book "someday" and today is that day. I consider this book my YOUlogy of sorts. What is my YOUlogy? It's my life story, my accomplishments and goals, my desires and dreams, and how and why I want to live my life full of passion and purpose. And that's where you come in. I want **YOU** to write—and live—your own YOUlogy.

My success and failures, hard knocks and good times, dreams and disappointments have filled the timeline of my life. Now that I'm committed to finally writing that book my audiences have been asking for, I do so with a purpose, passion and a vision for helping you to also succeed in life.

This book will help you not only appreciate the life you've led, but also get you to look forward to the life you've *yet* to lead. It will help get you "unstuck" from whatever rut you're currently grinding through, help you win whatever rat race you've been falling behind in and help you move your relationships—at work, at home and everywhere in between—further along than you ever thought possible. Most of all though, this book will get your mind off that early grave you've been digging and turn you toward a brighter future instead. So if you're ready to:

- make that change and live your passion,
- unleash all you have to offer on an unsuspecting world,
- get your blood pumping,
- and work smarter,

then you're ready to implement the six secrets in this book. You can start that new business, take a chance on a new relationship or turn your lackluster love life into something worthy of one of those *Fifty Shades* novels. Anything is possible. So yell out to the world, "I have arrived!" and then merely turn the page.

Your future, and your YOUlogy, is waiting for you there.

Introduction

The Six Secrets of Living Your YOUlogy

> *"Efforts and courage are not enough*
> *without purpose and direction."*
>
> **John F. Kennedy (1917–1963), Thirty-fifth U.S. President**
> **and youngest person ever elected to the U.S. Presidency**

I was giving a motivational speech at a synagogue in Long Island a few years ago and in the audience was a reporter from a local paper, *The Jewish Star.* Over the course of the next few days, she wrote several profiles about me for her paper.

As it turns out, the owner of a midsized publishing firm in Manhattan called K'tav Publishing which specializes in Jewish titles, read the articles. So he wrote me an e-mail that basically said, "Would you like to write a book?" Being a motivational speaker full of ideas to help inspire and motivate people, I shot back an almost immediate reply. "Heck yeah! Let's do this thing."

We met shortly afterward and apparently he liked my style enough to go into business with me. He sent over a contract, plus a small advance. Then nothing.

In the two years since, the only things I've written are two signatures. One when I signed the contract and the other when I endorsed the check. I have to assume that this man is either the most patient publisher in the world or he's merely moved on and forgotten about me.

However, then as now, I had every intention of writing that book. In fact, on multiple occasions my intent was to sit down and begin writing, but every time I did I just bailed. I couldn't stand looking at that blank sheet of paper and not finding anything to put on it.

So instead of actually writing, I busied myself with *how* to write. I watched videos on how to write, listened to tapes on how to write, read books on how to write, practiced writing exercises, read writing prompts and…none of it worked. Not a single thing.

The fact is that I love sharing, listening and speaking to people, but I *detest* writing. In fact, writing feels like a punishment to me. Here is what my internal dialogue sounds like when it's time to write: "Red, it's time to go in the corner and write. *Nooooo.* Please. Anything but writing."

I often wondered why I disliked writing so much until I remembered that when I was in middle school, if I misbehaved (yes, believe it or not, I misbehaved at times), I was required to write one hundred times, over and over again, either on the blackboard (back when there were such things as blackboards) or on a sheet of paper, such things as "I will do my homework on time" or "I will not flick rubber bands at the teacher's pet" or "I will not shoot spitballs at the teacher." You get the point.

Then, one day, when I was mentally trying to "shame" myself into writing, I discovered that, guess what: I didn't *have to* write. As I was moaning and kvetching one day, I ran across an article for a website that put authors, experts, speakers, coaches and consultants together with freelance professionals who could help edit, and even write, for and with them. I clicked the mouse a few times and, lo and behold, hit the mother lode.

There were hundreds of proven professionals on this website and, after speaking with a dozen or more, I found someone who could help me do what I do best without making me do all the legwork. My mantra in life has always been to "let the plumbers plumb and the painters paint."

I'm not good with plumbing, I make a mess of things whenever someone hands me a paintbrush and I don't like writing. Simple as that. So instead of waiting another two years for inspiration to strike, I hired someone who could turn my ideas into words and my dream, my YOUlogy, into reality. Consequently, here we are. So what's the point of this story?

My point is this. During those two years, as I struggled to find my voice and write page one of my own book, I learned the six secrets—and one bonus secret—you're about to discover. I also learned that they work in tandem.

One or two secrets aren't enough. They all need to work together if they're going to work at all.

So let's take a closer look and see how *The Six Secrets of Living Your YOUlogy* work together to help *you* lead a more productive, more inspired, happier and passion-filled life. First we will look at an overview of the six secrets and then we will examine each in detail in separate chapters.

The First Secret • *Identity* • *Knowing Who YOU Are*

Knowing who you are may seem like a no-brainer. "Who am I?" you may be asking yourself. "I'm me. That's who I am." But this secret goes deeper, *much deeper* than that.

We often think we're something we're not and we can live like that for years.

In fact, I told myself that I could be a successful businessman in a profession I wasn't really all that interested in. That is, until I just couldn't do it anymore and, when the business failed, I felt as if I had failed.

However, I was wrong. I hadn't failed. I just didn't know who I was yet and I subconsciously kept putting roadblocks in my own way to success.

Have you ever felt like that? Have you ever felt as if what you're doing day in and day out, or even who you're doing it with, is a lie? Think about how we approach adult life. Generally we go to high school, graduate and either a) go off to college and get a degree or b) start working right away.

Even with college in the mix, there is still a very narrow window in which we can choose what we want and love to do. Further, whether economic times are good or bad, the pressure to take the first job you get offered—any job—is great, especially if you owe the U.S. government $70,000 in student loans.

Now, I ask you, is that any way to find a dream job? Will that job taken out of desperation satisfy you emotionally, creatively, personally or even professionally? Will it allow you to live a passionate life and discover what you were really meant to do on this planet?

Hardly. Nonetheless, there you stay because there are bills to pay. You have mortgages, car loans, credit cards, the student debt and on and on. Still, we think we know ourselves because that is how we define ourselves. By our jobs.

"Who are you?"

"I'm a lawyer."

"No, who are you? What makes you happy or sad? What is your passion? What are your goals?"

"I…I'm a lawyer…"

"No, I'm not asking what you do to make money. Who are YOU? What makes your blood pump? What wakes you up excited every morning?"

"Um…I'm a lawyer? Um, I'm not sure?"

It's not that we don't care about who we *really* are. It's just that the more time we take to stop and examine our lives, the less time we have to live them. So our first secret will go a bit deeper. We'll work hard to uncover you, the *real* you, so that you can write your own YOUlogy and not someone else's.

The Second Secret • *Passion* • *Knowing What YOU Want*

This was an easy one for me. I knew what I wanted—to inspire others. See? Simple enough, right? Not quite. I had to learn all of the other secrets before I could put action to my passion and make it a reality.

I know a lot of people who struggle with this one. They just can't quite pin down why, exactly, they get out of bed in the morning.

- Is it to become a professional athlete?
- Is it to start a charity?
- Is it to write the Great American Novel?
- Is it to become a news anchor?
- Is it to be another Mother Teresa?
- Is it to appear in the most watched YouTube video?
- Is it to knit toilet paper covers shaped like southern belles?
- Is it to open an online store to sell flamingo Christmas ornaments?

The fact is, passion comes in many shapes and sizes and, in this day and age, you can literally make a living and a life out of nearly any passion you can imagine. So in the chapter on the second secret, we'll talk at length about how to find your passion and then what to do about it.

The Third Secret • *Time* • *Knowing When YOU Want It*

This one I learned the hard way. Timing really *is* everything which leads to my third secret, knowing when YOU want it. The fact is that if I had actually written this book two years ago when I signed that publisher's contract, God only knows what it would have sounded like. I simply wasn't ready.

However, that's OK. They say opportunity knocks only once, but when you make your own opportunities, it knocks all the time. In fact, opportunity will blow the door right off its hinges. *BOOM!*

Sometimes when we get things we're not quite ready for we waste an opportunity by fumbling the ball. However, when opportunity meets preparation, that's when real success occurs. For me, it took two years until I had not only mastered all six of these secrets, but also learned how to put them together. I recognized that now is the time to use what I know to help inspire others.

The Fourth Secret • *Power* • *Knowing How to Get It*

Having a goal or a set of goals is critically important, but the steps I needed to take to achieve this goal were one of the secrets that eluded me for the longest time. I knew what I wanted. I wanted to write a book. So, yes, that could be considered a goal, but what kept escaping me were the small-term daily, weekly and regular goals I needed to achieve that big goal.

I could see the book, its cover, my author's photo on the back and how multiple copies would look stacked up on a table during my first book signing. What I couldn't see was how to fill a blank page.

I couldn't see how to write a coherent outline and then begin to fill that in, chapter by chapter, page by page and even paragraph by paragraph. Those are the kinds of goals, the big ones and the small ones, we'll be discussing in the chapter on knowing how to get what you want.

The Fifth Secret • *Teamwork* • *The Buddy System*

This is a really important secret because you can go for months, and even years (as I did), if you're one of those people who believe that if you want it done right, you simply have to do it yourself. Take it from me, you don't—not anymore.

Whatever YOUlogy you want to live, there is someone out there just waiting to help you. If you want to start a new business, there are people who have done so and can help you learn from their mistakes. If you want that big promotion and it keeps eluding you, there are classes you can take to hone your skills or coaches you can hire for a few weeks or months to get you in business shape.

If you're having health issues, there are experts available that can get you the medical attention you need before it's too late. If you want a healthier relationship with your business partner, your significant other, etc., there are also experts who can help you achieve that goal too.

In the fifth secret, we'll talk about the importance of teamwork and what it means to truly tap into the creativity, expertise and enthusiasm of a like-minded individual, or even several individuals, who can help you achieve your goals.

The Sixth Secret • *Initiative* • *Knowing How to Get Started*

Getting started was really a hard one for me, as you may have gathered from my story at the beginning of this chapter. Even as the other secrets started to fall into place, even as I began to form a notion that writing this book was a goal I wanted to achieve, I was plagued by inertia. For months and months I struggled, until finally I was able to overcome the obstacles I had placed in my own path.

I couldn't start writing until I found someone to help me start writing. That was *my* starting line. Well, in the sixth secret, we'll help determine your own personal starting line by tackling the topic of initiative and how it's the glue that binds the rest of these secrets together.

*A **Bonus** Secret* • *Confidence* • *Knowing Your Worth*

I've listed knowing your worth as a "bonus" because it really works to supercharge the other six secrets. None of these secrets will work as effectively, or as purposefully, as you desire if you simply don't have the confidence that you deserve.

Whatever your YOUlogy is, be it getting that big promotion at work or simply finding work, whether it's proposing marriage or getting a divorce, writing your own book or musical or play or hit song, or overcoming a health, financial or emotional issue, if you don't feel that you're deserving, you'll never put any of the previous steps together.

As for myself, I really couldn't move forward with this book until I could look at myself in the mirror and ask, "What are you waiting for, Red? What's the *real* reason you're not writing your book?"

Only then would I realize what had really been holding me back was the fact that I didn't want it badly enough. The things I wanted—the things I couldn't live without—I always made happen. It dawned on me then that, as much as I said that I wanted to write a book, subconsciously I didn't *really* want to do so. Until now.

I finally understood that I wanted this book. I mean, I really, *really* wanted it. I was tired of people asking me, "Have you written a book?" and having to explain to them, "Well, um, see, I have a book '*contract*'…blah, blah, blah."

I was boring myself with all of my rationalizations as to why I hadn't written my book yet. However, when I finally got to the point of saying, "Okay, Red, no more excuses," that's when I was finally able to put the other six secrets together and make them happen.

So there you have them, the six secrets, plus one bonus secret, to writing your own YOUlogy. Now that you know what they're all about, it's time to start putting them to good use. That's what our next chapter, and our first "secret," will help you accomplish.

CHAPTER 1

The First Secret • Identity • Knowing Who YOU Are

"It is never too late to be what you might have been."
George Eliot (1819–1880), Female British writer

Knowing who you are isn't so much about "finding yourself" as it is about discovering yourself. I know the two seem similar, but as you'll find in the chapter ahead, there's actually quite a big difference.

Specifically, I think when people talk about finding themselves, what they're really talking about is finding what they'll do for a living. That's how most of us describe ourselves, isn't it? By what we do?

I mean, when you're at a cocktail party, nobody ever comes up to you and asks "Who are you?" (that is, unless you're crashing a wedding). Instead, they typically ask, "What do you do?"

I know that, for me, finding myself meant finding my place in the world—my career, my home, my family, my life. Going back even further to my youth, I know that my identity wasn't as much about finding myself as it was about finding my next job, my next twenty bucks, my next date, my next drink, my next "good time."

I call those years, say from my early twenties to early thirties my "automatic pilot" years. There was no real processing of data or emotions. It was all just kind of blindly stumbling forward, doing my own unique version of what I'd seen my parents do when I was growing up or what I saw my friends do as we all kept pace with each other on what we thought was the path to adulthood.

"Oh, shoot, Barry's working on Wall Street? Man, I better get my act together."

"What? Wally's married with a kid on the way? I don't want to get left behind."

"That's Chuck's house? Man, what's wrong with me? That guy must be doing all right."

So, subconsciously, you spend that very formative decade—your first decade as a real adult—following the cues and norms of your social circle. It is family first, close friends second, coworkers third and then acquaintances.

You graduated from high school, went to college, got a job, met someone, got married, settled down, bought a house and started having kids. And it's only really after that process, or your version of that process, when the dust settles and you find yourself nearing thirty (or just on the other side) and the house is quiet and the family's asleep, that you sit up in the middle of the night with the startling thought, "Hey, what about *me*? Where did my hopes and dreams go? Where did my *hair* go? What am I doing in this house and who are all these people making all this noise all the time?"

As for me, I'd always wanted to be an actor so I started reclaiming some of my own "life space" back as I began researching what made me happy instead of what just paid the bills. I felt a renewed sense of self and that's when I decided to write, act in and direct my own one-man show. Then, life got in the way. Or maybe I should say that I really started living.

Blue Pill or Red Pill: *Are You Still Living in the Matrix?*

In the hit movie *The Matrix*, Morpheus, played by Laurence Fishburne, gives Neo, played by Keanu Reeves, a choice: the blue pill or the red pill. If he swallows the blue pill, he can go about his business living the life of false security provided by the Matrix or that fake reality that everyone else lives. On the other hand, if he swallows the red pill, his eyes will be opened and he'll finally be "awake" to what life is really all about.

Blue pill = you live in denial of life's true reality.

Red pill = you wake up, face reality, and, in a sense, grow up.

For many years, I was an avid swallower of the blue pill. I got up every morning, went to work, provided and cared for my family, paid my taxes and figured the fastest way to the good life was to work myself half to death. Then, despite all my best intentions, all that hard work and playing by the "rules," life dealt me a series of staggering blows. I lost my job, I lost my marriage, I lost my family "unit" and I lost my home and security.

Walt Disney once famously said, "I think it's important to have a good hard failure when you're young. I learned a lot out of that." Now I know exactly what he meant.

Experiencing my newfound low was like finally taking the red pill and seeing that the rat race didn't have a finish line. I sat there, wallowing in my sad story, only to realize I was its author. *I* had written failure into my biography—my YOUlogy—because I hadn't really gone after what I'd wanted.

I had lost sight of my passion. It was buried so deeply, I didn't even know if it existed anymore. I was pursuing only what society told me were the "right" things to want. A job, security, home, family, stability and a paycheck (with the eventual social security and death).

It's funny because I had always wanted to be an actor and it turned out that I'd been "acting" all my life by playing the part of someone I really wasn't. I was conforming to ideas, situations and scenarios I simply didn't believe in and that weren't authentic to my true journey or my true self.

The Gift of Self: *Life's Big "Do Over."*

Although, at the time it was the lowest point in my life, today I refer to my dark days as a gift. Why? Because they woke me up, shook me out of my slumber and forced me to open my eyes to the reality that it wasn't all about me.

I was put on this earth for a purpose and that wasn't just to take up space at a job I didn't care about, hating myself, my life, and those around me because I was so miserable and unhappy. Losing it all gave me the chance to start over from scratch, to get a giant "do over" in life and replay the game from level one.

I suddenly had a blank slate and nowhere to go but up. So I joined a men's group where my friend, innocently enough, asked me about becoming a motivational speaker. Here was a chance to do what I was *really* passionate about—making the world a better place.

What's more, I could take the skills I'd been developing in my acting classes over the years and put them to good use when I was in front of people. During the process I would listen to their cues, pick them up when they were down and rev them up if their energy level lagged. I could build my presentation to a crescendo to really tap into their emotions and provide a rousing finish to send them off happier, healthier and more motivated.

Your Own Personal Evolution: *Don't Just Get There, Be There.*

The best thing I've learned about myself is that I am not done yet. My journey to self is just that—a journey. I am on it and that is the greatest place to be, no matter how much I earn or don't earn, where I live or don't live or what's in my bank account.

Now when I go to a cocktail party, I no longer offer the standard answer when people ask me what I do. I am confident enough to say, "It's not what I *do* that's important. What matters most is my passion. I don't want to know what you *do*. I want to know who you are and I'm happy to share who I am." Those are the types of conversations that make my blood pump the fastest. Why? Because they're real.

What's more, being happier with myself has made me better in everything else I do. I'm a better husband, a better ex-husband, a better father, a better brother and son, a better speaker, friend, neighbor and, generally, a better person. Am I perfect? Far from it. But I've given myself permission to be imperfect. Today I am striving for "better" and that is plenty perfect enough for me.

What We Do Is *Not* Who We Are.

No one, and I mean not even the biggest workaholic, is defined by his or her job. Take a guy like Stephen

King, who churns out more words per day than most word processors, and he is *still* so much more than an author. He is a husband and father, he's in a rock band, he writes articles about publishing and technology and he is a vibrant supporter of other authors.

He is a neighbor and, by all accounts, an extremely generous and charitable individual who happens to write. He has interests, hobbies, relationships, passions and pursuits over and above what he does to earn a living.

Even someone like Barack Obama is not defined by his job description. He too is a husband, a father, a colleague and a friend. He is a mentor to many and an inspiration to many more. One day, when he leaves office after his second term, he, like Bill Clinton and George W. Bush, will have to readjust to civilian life and follow those pursuits that, perhaps, he's put on hold for eight years.

Even if we're not best-selling authors, politicians, big-time celebrities, movers and shakers or heads of state, what we do does not necessarily define *us* either. Most people do what they do for a living because of one simple reason. It brings home a paycheck.

If you're a medical doctor and you feel that you've found your calling, that's an amazing gift, to be paid to do what you love. That's how I feel. I love speaking to people, helping them see life from a different perspective and getting paid to do it. In fact, I'd do it for free.

What Would You Do for Free?

Seriously, if money were no object, I would absolutely, positively and voluntarily speak and inspire for free. I believe most people who love what they do feel the same. So the question you have to ask yourself is, "What would I do for free?"

Would you balance the books at your local grocery store for free? Would you teach for free? Would you work as a nurse for free? Would you mow lawns, or sell shoes or Bibles door-to-door, for free?

If nothing comes to mind at first, dig deeper and ask again, "What would I do for free?" Part of knowing ourselves is knowing our passion. It is feeling free to ask deeper questions and buck the status quo, or maybe even making big changes so that we can get paid to do what we love. First, however, you have to find what you love and that's just what this next section is intended to help you accomplish.

The Starting Line Is Here: *Five Steps to Knowing Yourself Better.*

What would life be like if you were comfortable in your own skin? What would it be like if you could answer the question "Who are you?" with more than what you do for a living? As part of our journey toward a higher level of self-awareness, let's go through a series of five steps and see how they can help you find out more about yourself so that you can get more out of your life.

The First Step • *Hit the "Pause" Button.*

So often our lives are moving so fast that it's almost impossible to stop the daily commute, the endless meetings, conference calls and deadlines to simply sit back, take a deep breath and say, "Where do I go from here?"

During the time when my life was close to rock bottom, I suffered with anxiety that would wake me up every single morning. I would love the nighttime before I went to sleep because, at that time of the day, I felt fine. I felt like I could handle the breakup of my marriage, the stress around money and making ends meet. I could control my thoughts while I was awake, holding the anxiety at bay during the day.

At night though, while I was sleeping, it seemed like my subconscious took over and the anxiety would continue to grow until it got strong enough to wake me up. I would open my eyes and lay there, my body tingling and filled with fear. I dreaded the morning.

Sometimes I would walk to my kids' room to look at them while they were sleeping and that would give me some strength. Other days, I was so scared that I would lie on my bathroom floor, curled up like a fetus and cry. I felt like there was no way out.

I'd always believed in God and I was a devout man. I even attended synagogue every Saturday for services. So, many mornings, when the anxiety was overwhelming, I would go into my living room, face the wall to the east, and pray.

I'd recite two psalms over and over again and cry to God, literally begging him to help me. "Help me get through the day, the minutes and the seconds. Please take away this anxiety. Please save me."

I would open my *siddur*, my prayer book, and I would turn to Psalm 121 and recite it in Hebrew. *Shiur hamaalos esau enau al haarim maayin yavo ezri.* Then I would recite it in English, a song of ascents:

> *"I will lift up mine eyes unto the mountains, from whence shall my help come? My help cometh from the Lord, who made heaven and earth. The Lord shall keep thee from all evil. He shall keep thy soul. The Lord shall guard thy going out and thy coming in, from this time forth and forever."*

I would recite it again and again, facing that the wall, pleading "I need your help, God. I don't know where else to turn!" The apartment would be quiet and everyone else would be asleep, and I would just continue to look at the wall and cry, repeating those two psalms over and over. I still remember that wall like it was yesterday. It was an off-gold color.

Looking back I've realized that, as I was praying to God, I was also giving myself strength to start the day... one foot in front of the other, one step at a time. My faith served as a wonderful tool as it centered me. It gave me that little sliver of hope that I could make a new life for myself.

So the first step to getting to know yourself better is to simply hit the mental "pause" button on your life and center yourself. It involves going into your mind and heart, the place where you're most deeply attuned to yourself as a part of nature and of the universe, and getting to the most fundamental "you" that exists.

Start thinking about who you are more closely. Leave your smartphone or tablet at home, find a quiet place like a local park or bookstore, buy yourself a cup of coffee and think about yourself for a change.

Don't think about what's wrong with yourself or how much money you owe or which project you should be working on or which deadline you're probably going to miss. Just think about *you*. Give yourself permission to ask the questions that need to be asked, to ponder where you are, where you're going and where you want to go.

You don't need to do anything formal here. Just stop to think about your life. The more you think about it, the more you'll know if you're close to where you want to be—or if you're miles and miles away.

The Second Step • *Start Looking.*

You'll never be able to "find yourself" if you don't send out a search party. In other words, if you don't feel like you have a good handle on who you are, then your first course of action is to start looking for your true identity.

You want to make this a priority now, while you're reading this book, while you're motivated and feeling good about the prospect of making some serious changes in your life. You want to not only get to know yourself better, but to also feel better, be happier and help others more.

Again, a good way to start is to simply ask more questions, probe more deeply and use your quiet moments to continue searching for the answers. It doesn't have to happen overnight, but you'll never find yourself if you never start looking.

The Third Step • *Ask Tough Questions.*

It is *imperative* to ask yourself the tough questions, the penetrating questions, if you ever want to get to the source of why you might be frustrated enough to pick up a book called *Live Your YOUlogy.*

- What am I doing wrong?
- What am I doing right?
- What do I like about my life?
- What do I dislike about my life?
- Where am I going?

- Am I headed in the right direction?
- Am I happy?
- Am I sad?
- Are my physical problems—anxiety, headaches, stress, stomachaches, or lack of sleep—a disease or simply symptoms of my dissatisfaction?
- How can I change?
- Do I already know what needs to be done and am I just too afraid to do it?

The only way to move forward is to center yourself. You must pause, stopping your progress completely, look in the mirror and answer truthfully the tough questions you know you've wanted to ask your whole life. You never know, you might be surprised by the answers you give yourself.

Whenever I do this exercise in my seminars, a lot of people really respond to that last question, "Do I already know what needs to be done and am I just too afraid to do it?" Most of us, if we're honest, know our lives are not perfect. We live, we work, we earn and we go through the motions because, well, there's this house to pay for and two cars in the garage and little Bobby needs braces and Jenny will be going to Dartmouth in a few years and it's been a while since we've gone on a family vacation, so there's that big cruise coming up and…and…amidst it all, we still know life's not quite "right."

We're going through the motions but we're not hitting our stride. Things are "okay" but they're not "great" and we desperately want them to be great. The difference between good and great is often in the little things, such as the steps we take, the questions we ask, the answers we give and, most importantly, the honesty of the answers.

If you are unhappy, doing the same things that made you that way won't make you any happier. Only when you change your course will you change the destination. First, however, you have to know where you *want* to go and that starts with your willingness to ask the tough questions and give honest answers.

The Fourth Step • *Get Educated.*

One of the first things I did when I started to get my life back in gear was to read. I read *What Color Is Your Parachute?* by Richard N. Bolles, the default book for those seeking to find their passion or reinvent their lives. In addition, I was truly inspired by Po Bronson's *What Should I Do with My Life? The True Story of People Who Answered the Ultimate Question.*

I was also blessed to have the insight offered by my men's group. The meetings really opened my eyes and helped me look at life differently, to take action and, above all, to get involved. I took part as often as I could on weekend retreats, night classes, brown bag talks and morning meetings. Whenever possible, I seized the opportunity to gain knowledge or connect with others who might mentor or help me.

Be hungry for knowledge and get excited about that one connection, that one mentor or coach or boss or colleague, or whomever. It's a big help to have someone who will ask you the right questions or challenge you in just the right way, at just the right time, to kick you off on your own journey to self-discovery.

If my friend Mark had never suggested that I explore becoming a motivational speaker, if I hadn't gotten out of my brother's basement, if I hadn't joined that men's group, if I hadn't gotten involved and made myself open and available to that kind of suggestion, I might not be writing these words today.

The Fifth Step • *Take Action.*

Finally, take action. Get to know yourself better by doing something—anything.

- Take a class.
- Read a book.
- Go to a seminar.
- Go on a retreat with a motivational speaker or guru.
- Seek out educational opportunities.
- Go away by yourself, for yourself.
- Find a life coach.
- Join a local support, men's, or women's group.

- Start paying down your debt so you can pursue a lower paying but more satisfying job.

It's vital that you do something, even though it may not provide results tomorrow. For instance, if you know your current job isn't making you happy but you have a spouse and kids to support and a mortgage and bills to pay, you can't just cut ties, burn your bridges and get lost, can you?

Instead, be open with yourself and with your spouse and discuss your options. See what ways you can start to save, eliminate some expenses or "crunch the numbers" so that you can within a given time frame—six months, one year or maybe even two years—phase out of your job completely and start doing something you truly love.

Maybe, while you're paying down your debt or making other arrangements, you can take a class, refine your skills or otherwise prepare yourself for the career shift so that this period doesn't feel like "lost" time to you and your family. Whatever you do, you must do *something* if you are ever to make a change.

Perhaps the change won't be as drastic as a job switch or uprooting your family to move across the country. However, if you're reading this, then you must want something or some things in your life to be different. You must be feeling (like I did up until a few years ago) that something is missing and that *you*, not any *one* or any *thing* else, are the missing link. In that case, even if all you do is read this book and think slightly differently, you are at least doing something to bring yourself into greater focus and that's a start.

Life in the *Red* Zone: *Parting Words about Knowing Yourself.*

Knowing yourself is just one more step on the path to living your YOUlogy, but it's a vital step because it's the first step. I've said it before, but it bears repeating, I couldn't have written this book if I didn't know enough about myself to have something to say.

Ten years ago, five years ago, even two years ago, I just wasn't sufficiently in touch with myself to realize how critical creating this book would be to my growth (and to yours too, I hope!). At that time, I couldn't find the words to convince you how important knowing yourself is to your journey to self-fulfillment and living your YOUlogy.

Now I'm ready. Are you?

CHAPTER 2

The Second Secret • Passion • Knowing What YOU Want

*"The man who does things makes mistakes,
but he never makes the biggest mistake of all—doing nothing."*
**Benjamin Franklin (1706–1790), Statesman, scientist
and one of America's founders**

My divorce and bankruptcy made one thing about what I wanted very clear to me. I wanted to be a father to my kids and that was an area of my life that I was not willing to compromise, no matter what it meant for me. I wanted my children to live as "normal" a life as possible and to be close to them. They were my world and if that meant that my lifestyle had to change too, so be it.

Initially, I lived in the basement of my brother, Sam's house. It was about a forty-minute train ride to the city so I could be somewhat close to my kids. I slept on one bed in the room and my clothes, my only belongings, were piled neatly on the other bed.

During that time, my good friend Tehillah let me crash at her apartment a few weekdays and weekends. About a month or two later, my friend Elliot let me move into his apartment in the city. This allowed me to be closer to my children and to see them more often. The one thing I wanted more than anything.

Elliot's apartment was unfurnished as it was on the market, so I bought a couple of air mattresses so my kids could sleep over and a folding table and chairs from my parents so we could eat together. It wasn't the nine-room apartment we'd shared before, but I was within walking distance of their apartment, and we could easily be together more often.

I was able to live at Elliot's place for about two months until it was sold. In the meantime though, I had asked around and was able to find a small two-bedroom apartment on Ninety-Sixth Street, about five blocks from where my kids were living with their mom.

I didn't have a lot of money so I went to Ikea and bought them a bunk bed, some other inexpensive furniture and household utensils. I did the best I could to make it a home.

The divorce was hard on my kids and they didn't usually sleep over. They would come over for dinner and, when it was over, I would walk them back home.

I went from having a home filled with my children's laughter to a quiet, empty apartment. I felt a huge void every time I dropped them off.

It was very challenging for me as my visions of fatherhood were being turned upside down. How could I be the father I wanted to be when I wasn't with my kids? It was a life I never envisioned could, or would, happen to me.

I stayed in that place for about two years, or until I couldn't afford it anymore. My residence options had shrunk dramatically and none of them were very appealing. I could go back to court and ask to reduce my alimony, but then my kids couldn't live in the city, near their friends and school. I could also go back to my brother or even live at my parents' house, which is what I chose to do.

In hindsight, that was the best and worst choice all wrapped into one. Door-to-door, my commute was over an hour-and-a-half on the bus each way *and* I had to find a place in the city to sleep on the nights that I could see my children. I was constantly carrying an overnight bag.

When we were together though, we would visit the local Starbucks, Dunkin' Donuts and pizza shops, basically anywhere we could sit and talk. During those very trying times, I realized what a strong support system I had built around me. My friends would let me stay over, most times at a moment's notice. My parents, with their unconditional love, accepted me with open arms.

Although it was terribly hard as an adult with my own children to move back into my parents' house, I was blessed that I had a way to regroup and stabilize my finances. It was just what I needed.

The intolerable bus ride back and forth every day gave me the determination to find another place in the city to live. After only three months, another friend came to my rescue.

Meryl, whom I'd known for about twenty years and had considered a sister (she even has red hair like me), had a two-bedroom apartment that she'd let me crash at some nights. So I asked her if I could be her housemate. She agreed to test it out and, after about a month, she decided to let me stay for good.

It was her openness and willingness to work with me that allowed me to be near my kids and to stay connected with them at such a critical time in their lives. They had a place to sleep over, to eat or to just hang out with me. I was near my synagogue, work *and* my children…and it was all within my budget.

Since I didn't have the quantity of time with my children that I desired, I had to really focus on the quality of time we would spend together. I would shut off my phone and focus entirely on being present with them. Through these challenges, I knew that I would do anything to stay in my kids' lives—no matter what.

They always came first and I made sure they knew that. I kept an open dialogue with them as I wanted them to know they were always with me in my heart and soul and that they could reach out to me anytime, anywhere. I wanted them to know I loved them unconditionally.

I had my phone on every night in case they needed me for any reason and I'm so glad that I made them my priority because doing so fortified our love for each other and built an even stronger foundation for our relationship. We began sharing our feelings, our thoughts and our challenges with each other.

I couldn't have dreamt of developing better, closer or more loving relationships with my children. I needed to learn how to be the best dad I could be from afar, so I treasured the times we were together. Now we share our feelings with one another; we communicate on a daily basis and our lives are filled with love and blessings.

The choices were tough, but the payoff has been extraordinary. My ability to remain a part of my children's lives, in the face of so many obstacles, has taught me that when we identify what we most want—what we call our "true passion"—we are unstoppable!

I speak to a lot of groups and whenever I ask people what their "passion" is, I am invariably greeted with rows of blank faces staring back at me. This reaction troubles me because those I speak to are what I call "established." They are executives, white-collar workers, professionals and mothers and fathers with mortgages, homes and kids, and yet they don't have any idea what their "passion" looks like.

They might have known once upon a time as they may have had dreams, in high school or college, about being a veterinarian or raising plants or playing professional basketball or writing catchy commercial jingles or hit songs. But life sucked the passion out of them at some point. I know it sucked it out of me.

For many years, I was simply not alive. I was going through the motions, zombie-like. One of my most popular speeches is actually called "Zombies" and I think it's popular because people can really relate to the idea of going through life on autopilot. They can understand that type of situation because we've all done it, often for years and years and years.

Take the Curvy Path: *At Least You're Moving Forward.*

My own path to finding my passion was curvy, to say the least. I always thought I wanted to be an actor who would read someone else's words from a script and project them to an adoring audience. When no one would write a script for me or hire me to read theirs, I wrote my own and put on my own show.

However, when that failed to place me on the national stage, when people failed to respond to my attempts to do what I thought I loved, it threw me for a loop. *Maybe my heart wasn't in it,* I thought. *Maybe people saw that.*

Like most actors, I had to get a day job and I was miserable. Nonetheless, I went through the routine, zombie-like, one of the living dead, with my head down, shuffling to and from work every day just to provide my family with the necessities of life.

I didn't know my passion then. I just knew I wanted out. So when my out came in the form of a perfect storm of emotional, professional and financial ruin, it gave me a "do over" of sorts. When you're at rock bottom, the only place to go is up, right?

My crisis provided me with a unique opportunity to contemplate what I wanted. Even then, it still took the suggestion made by Mark before I realized that I had other options.

And although I was excited by the prospect of an exciting new career, I had a slew of reservations. I had been taught that sitting at a desk, clocking in from nine to five every day and getting a steady paycheck, was my lot in life. Don't we all think that?

Even in the midst of my passion, as the ember started to glow within me more and more brightly with each passing day, I kept pouring cold water on it with my own doubts, fears, anxieties and preconceived notions about what it meant to earn a living and to go to work. What it meant to "be a man."

Eventually I gave in to the temptation to follow my passion and I began my journey to discovering what my heart really wanted. For my first few speeches, someone had to literally drag me onto the stage, but once I got there I knew I was in the right spot.

As cards and letters of appreciation came pouring in, some of them even making me cry, that dying ember of passion buried deep inside didn't just get hot again. It was as if it had gasoline poured on it and the flames flared high into the sky. You couldn't keep me from getting back onstage back then and you can't keep me off it now.

That smoldering ember inside you, that childhood passion you buried so long ago, needs air to breathe. You need to bring it out of the deep, dark pit of your chest and give it sunlight. You need to show it to the world and fan those flames so that it will never fade again.

Your Flame Isn't Gone: *It's Just on Life Support.*

The good news about passion is that, while you're still alive, it never ever goes out entirely. Therefore, your job is to get it going again before it's too late. To begin that process, I have some questions for you:

- What's your passion?
- What do you want to do with your life?
- How do you want to live your life?
- How are you going to wake up every day and say, "I love what I'm doing! I love my life. This is what I was meant to do!"?
- What do you want your legacy to be?

What finally woke me up to my passion was when I started really seeing the masses walking around New York City, eyes on the ground, marching in step, just like... well, zombies. Moreover, I saw the same thing in myself.

I saw the same people doing the same things every single day. We're riding on the subway. We're walking down the street. We're waiting in line for a cup of coffee. We're funneling down the escalator on our way to work.

We don't even smile. It seems as if we *can't* smile. We are so focused that we are almost in a trance. It almost seems as if we have blinders on. That's because we have just two thoughts in our heads:

- Gotta pay the bills.
- Gotta go to work.
- Gotta pay the bills.
- Gotta go to work.
- Gotta pay the bills.
- Gotta go to work.
- Gotta go to work.
- Gotta go to work.
- Gotta go to work.
- *Gotta go to work*!

And for what?

For the money?

We're doing it for the *money*? Is that *it*? This is capitalist America. People come from all over the world to make a quick buck. This is the land of opportunity. But wait. Do we really think that money will make our lives happier? Do we think that it will make our lives easier? Well, let's see, shall we?

By that reasoning, we need to make more money

- to buy better clothes,
- to move up in our careers, and
- to buy a nicer car, which earns us the privilege of higher car payments.

Then we have to work sixty-hour weeks just to pay *those* bills, which means spending less time with our families, however, we do it

- so we can make even more money,
- so we can buy an even bigger house, which just means we go further into debt,
- so we can become head manager and work one hundred twenty hours a week just to make ends meet.

Unfortunately, this rat race just keeps going and going and going and *going*. Where does it end?

One day, I stopped in the middle of my tracks, turned around, put up my hands and yelled, "*Stop*! Turn around. *Go home.* Go home to your families. You do not want to be doing this. You do not want to spend the next fifty years doing this. Just. Go. Home!"

Okay, fine. So I didn't really say that to *everyone* in midtown Manhattan. Still, I wanted to. I really did. Instead, I said it to myself, and that's probably one of the most important conversations I've ever had.

The Backward Guide to Life.

When it comes to work and life balance, we actually have it all backward. Whoever made up this calendar thing really put it in reverse. We work five days of the week just so we can spend two days with our families. Wouldn't it make more sense to work two days a week and be able to spend five days enjoying life with the ones we love? I think so.

Yes, I used to be a zombie. Then one day I said to myself (I actually said this), "*Red, stop! Stop this non-sense. You do not want to live this life.*"

And that's what I'm here to share with you today. If I have the power to make the change, so do you. Yes, we all have many responsibilities. I have mine—children, tuition, alimony payments, rent, food, etc.—however these are just excuses I could make to avoid change. Excuses I don't want you to make either.

Pretend That You're Dead: *What Will People Say About You After You're Gone?*

So let's put all of our excuses to the side and start with a blank slate. Do you want a meaningful life? Are you ready to do what you love to do…what you were *meant* to do?

Here's my tool for you: Pretend that you're dead. That's right. Write your own eulogy, your *YOUlogy*, by asking yourself, "What would I like people to say about me at my funeral?" Would it be about:

- How early I went to work?
- How much time I spent with my kids?
- How much overtime I put in?
- How much I volunteered for my community?

- How I closed that big deal?
- How I took care of my parents?
- How many cars I owned?
- How I drove my neighbor to the supermarket when she was too sick to drive herself?

I think you get the drift. After you write your YOUlogy, look at it and study it closely. What matters most to you will likely look a bit different as this exercise will shift your energy, allowing your new understanding to really envelop you. You'll more easily realize what matters most—and what doesn't.

Are You One of the Living or One of the Living Dead?

Coming back into the world of the living starts with baby steps—tiny little steps. Ever since writing my own YOUlogy, I make the time to look inside myself, to understand myself and then to work on improving myself. As I said, it's the little things that separate the living from the living dead.

If a train is overcrowded, I wait for the next one. I'm a person, not a sardine… *"Red was a patient man."*

I smile and say "Good morning." I mean, everyone loves a smile, right? I've got one, so might as well share it… *"It was always great to see Red. He always had a smile on his face."*

If someone is running for the elevator, I don't pretend to look for the open door button and give him or her my "I can't help you" face. You know what I'm talking about. Instead, I hold it open for them. After all, if I don't have an extra five seconds in my life to do a nice thing (and that's all it takes to hold the door open, five seconds), if I can't take that five seconds for a fellow human being, then I'm pathetic… *"Red always held the elevator door for people. He was so nice."*

I make the time to connect with my friends, my family and my children. I give them my full attention by turning off my iPhone (yes, believe it or not, it has an off switch)… *"Red always made time for me and paid full attention to me. He was a great and caring friend. I knew I could always count on him."*

These are some of the baby steps. The bigger steps? I have taken the time to discover what I was meant to do in my life and why I was put on this earth. I have figured out what gets my blood pumping and it is helping people discover what *they* were meant to do with their lives and inspiring them to do it. That is exactly what I'm doing now—helping people to live the lives they were meant to live.

We all have the power within ourselves to break the mold, to get out of the rut, to get off the subway. My suggestion to you is that if you're ready to make a change, if you're ready to start living your life, start with the baby steps. I shared my baby steps with you, so feel free to use them or discover your own.

The quicker you start with the first step, the quicker you will be on your way to living to your full potential. So here's to living your passion and the life you were meant to live!

Bonus Activity: *The Money Test.*

Really, it all comes down to money. I think the need for money is what keeps people from trying to live their passion. It is a huge influence in all of our lives, even when we don't want it to be. So when people tell me they are struggling with figuring out what they love, I always say to them, "Let's take money out of the equation."

This is a little activity I do at my speaking engagements to help people find their passion. It works for a lot of them, and I hope it works for you.

If I were to give you, say, an extra $500, what would you do with it? If you're like most people, you'd pay down your debt, or get your car fixed, or take care of some much-needed business you've been putting off until you could "save up."

Maybe you'd even treat yourself to a weekend getaway, some clothes you've been waiting to buy until they went on sale, some school supplies for the kids or maybe you'd open a savings account if you don't already have one.

Say I give you another $1,000 on top of the first $500. Not instead of, on top of. Now you've done whatever you were going to do with the first $500 *and* you have an extra grand to play around with. Now what would you do? Think of the opportunities that come to mind.

Now I'm going to give you another $2,000 on top of the $1,500 I've already given you. At this point, you're in major treat territory. You've gotten rid of some basic needs, maybe gotten the brakes fixed on your car, paid off the last installments on your student loan or paid for your oldest child's braces, so now it's splurge time.

Perhaps you take those dance classes you've always wanted to take but could never afford. Or maybe you learn to play the piano, something you've always wanted to try and thought you might be good at.

Then, the next week, I turn around and give you $5,000. Wow! So you take a month off from work to dance full time or invest in a secondhand piano to practice and really learn how to play.

Now let me lay $50,000 on you. Fifty grand. That's more than some people make in a year. What could you do with $50,000? I mean, you've already started a savings account, taken care of a lot of basic needs and even treated yourself to some vacations and "bucket list" items you've always wanted to try. Now what?

However, let's not stop there. Say the following week I give you $500,000. That's life changing money right there, but I'm just getting started. Let's say, once and for all, I hand you $1,000,000 free and clear. No taxes, no duties, no crossed fingers, no strings attached.

So with the $500,000, you pretty much said goodbye to your old life and with the one million dollars you can start a new one. Now what would you do? We've taken money out of the equation, so now you're free to do anything and everything your heart desires.

While we're talking about money, let's say I drop in with a big box with a bow on top and say, "I'm feeling generous. Here's an extra $5,000,000 on top of everything else I've already given you."

Now you are literally unencumbered by cash. You've paid off your mortgage, your cars, your student loans and your credit cards. Your kids have college funds, your 401(k) and IRA accounts are stuffed to the gills, and you've got money in the bank. You've even quit your job. So, now what?

If you took money out of your personal equation, took a month off and woke up one morning wanting to contribute to society again without having to worry about a paycheck, what would you do?

That thing you lean toward, that joy you feel in your heart—dancing, playing piano, helping people, being a motivational speaker, acting or starting your own sneaker factory—that is your passion.

You may want to buy some land in Alaska, escape the rat race altogether, and build a log cabin from scratch. It may be tough, sweaty work, leaving blisters on your hands and corns on your feet, but it may also bring you back to life.

That thing you *love* to do, that thing no one can keep you away from once you start doing it, that thing you'd do for free if money weren't an issue—that's your passion. That's what will turn you from one of the living dead back into one of the living.

CHAPTER 3

The Third Secret • Time • Knowing When YOU Want It

"If not now, *when?"*
Hillel (30 BC–AD 10), Jewish scholar

Every so often we experience defining moments. By "defining" I mean those little life moments that stop you in your tracks and force you to reevaluate or even redesign your entire life. They are those 'a-ha' flashes when you push the pause button on whatever it is you've been doing and realize that you're going in the wrong direction, or possibly just standing still.

What's great about defining moments is that they're really what I call opportunities in disguise. They allow you to step back, reassess, reevaluate and press forward in a new, bolder, better or simply differ-ent direction.

In other words, like big, beefy extras in a mobster movie, defining moments grab you by the lapels, slap you around a little bit and shout in your face "This is the time! What are you doing? Stop wasting time and get on with your life!"

It's All Good (Or Is It?)

We rarely have a defining moment when life is "all good." Instead, they usually occur when we're on a kind of emo-tional autopilot, drifting through life, playing by the rule book we've written for ourselves—or, perhaps, that's been written by our circumstances.

Don't get me wrong. When life is genuinely and purposefully good because you've created it to be that way, it is great—authentically, awesomely great. Oftentimes, however, we talk ourselves into *thinking* our life is good when really it's just okay, average or even just familiar. Maybe we think that because we just bought that big house, or put in a pool, or got a pro-motion, or moved into a higher tax bracket or better neighborhood.

I know this all too well because I was on autopilot for years, drifting through my job and family life, going along to get along, winding up in a really nice Upper

West Side apartment in New York City and wondering how, exactly, I'd gotten there.

There's a famous Yiddish expression I use when looking back on this time of my life: *Nisht ahein un Nisht ahair.* It means "neither here nor there." Indeed, I wasn't here and I wasn't there. Wherever I was, I wanted to be somewhere else.

When I was at work, I wanted to be home. When I was at home, I wanted to be back at work. If we were at a nice dinner, I'd wonder what I'd be doing tomorrow. It wasn't so much a reflection of who I was with at the time, but how I was spending my time in the first place.

I wasn't happy, but I didn't know it because I had been taught that what I had at the time—the job, the apartment, the wife, the kids, the summer house—was supposed to make you happy. I had it all; therefore I must be happy about it all.

It's often during these "good" times, these "neither here nor there" times, when we get inklings of unrest or dissatisfaction and don't quite know what to do with them. They aren't anything overt, maybe just general feelings of malaise.

My Defining Moment: *A Line in the Sand.*

I can remember exactly where I was when a major defining moment happened for me. I was standing in a doorway on Tenth Avenue and Twenty-Eighth Street in Manhattan. That particular instant, I couldn't get any lower.

I was divorced and hadn't seen my kids in days. I had no money and nowhere to live. Depressed, anxious and uncertain, I had no direction and nothing was happening. Aside from my health, I had nothing really.

I'm not sure why I crumbled right then. Minutes earlier I'd been just another city dweller—walking around, looking, talking and acting like everybody else. Then, suddenly, it hit me all at once and I couldn't take another step. I ended up leaning in a strange doorway crying, a shell of my former self.

I couldn't stand the pain anymore; it was unbearable. So I thought of running away and starting completely over. I had nothing there in the city holding me back— no wife, no house, no job. Why should I stay? Then much darker thoughts intruded.

I could find a car and drive into the Hudson River. I could end it all, the pain, the humiliation of losing everything and the hard, humbling work of starting all over again to attempt to get it back. I'm not saying I would have done it, but at that moment, if I were ever going to do it, I *could* have done it right then.

I was in the abyss of a deep hole that was too dark to walk around in and too high to climb back out of. What brought me back from it, what finally made me see the light at the end of the tunnel, were my three kids.

I might not have been "Father of the Year" at that very moment, but they needed me, and I needed them.

We needed to be in each other's lives for the good times and the bad. At least I knew enough, thank God, not to make a permanent decision in a temporary moment of weakness.

I saw the faces of my children and smiled for the first time in I don't know how long. I knew then that running away from my problems wasn't the answer. Instead, I had to find a way to face them, to start over, to make something more of my life than just sitting around in my brother's basement, battling depression or crying in strangers' doorways.

That was *my* defining moment, and it was a doozy. I didn't leave that doorway with my passion in place, but I definitely left it knowing one thing. It was up to me to change my life. No one was going to do it for me. No superhero was going to come and rescue me. To quote the famous line from *The Shawshank Redemption*, I needed to "get busy living or get busy dying."

Embrace Challenge: *Now is the Time.*

I'm not saying I had to hit rock bottom to find my passion or start all over again but, for me, that moment provided a sense of clarity that was missing when things were "going well" in my life. It was like God had just ripped the blinders off and allowed me to see my life for what it really was, without the rose-colored glasses. I *had* to have that experience.

I truly hope that you don't find yourself at the bottom of a deep hole, God knows I don't wish my rock bottom on my worst enemy, but I had to experience all of it—divorce, business failure, bankruptcy, depression, homelessness, all of it—before I could see the truth of *my* life and start all over again from scratch.

So I repeat that, typically, it's not when life is really good that we make life changes, it's when we're down. That's why there is nothing like a difficult challenge to force you out of the rut that you're in and drive you to do something that changes your life for the good.

Doing something differently may sound like no big deal but, when you think about it, there are a lot of things you probably do (or don't do) that you're not really very willing to do another way. However, I can't urge you strongly enough to allow yourself to be open-minded when it comes to making changes in your life.

For example, I was not someone who took drugs for mental-health purposes. Not me. Not doing it. But I was in therapy at the time and I remember a session in which I cried and described the huge pool of sadness inside of me. And I felt like I could control it if I just added more therapy sessions. Perhaps if I went two or three times a week, I could "fix" myself.

My therapist told me that my anxiety was probably an expression of depression and she wanted to send me to a pharmacologist who could prescribe medication. I looked at her like she was the one who needed therapy. I didn't need any drugs to feel better. I was a powerful man and I could handle my problems on my own. I just needed more sessions to work my way through what I was experiencing. She refused, gave me the pharmacologist's number and told me to call him.

Being a dutiful patient, I made the appointment. When I met with him, he asked me a series of questions and told me I was a perfect candidate for antidepressants. The meds would help me, he said, but I told him I didn't want any. My life was crumbling and I was an emotional mess, and yet, I was so stubborn that I thought I could handle it all without drugs. In retrospect, I must have been in an altered state.

I accepted that if I broke my leg the doctor would put it in a cast and that if I had a problem with my eyesight then I might need glasses, but I also believed that if my emotions weren't working properly, I could "fix" them myself. "Just take the prescription," he said, "and at least you have it if you want it." I carried it around in my pocket for probably two weeks before the pain and sadness sent me to the drugstore. I went back to the doctor and told him I was ready to take the medication. I'm so happy that I did.

"Admitting" that my depth of unhappiness warranted taking medication was a big challenge for me. It was a defining moment to the extent that I realized I had to be open to events and actions that I had previously considered untenable.

Some challenges will be more compelling than others. For instance, getting a flat tire may be a difficulty that you face, but depending on where you are in life, it may or may not lead to a defining moment.

You could get that flat tire on the way to pick up your $40,000,000 check at the lottery office, on the way to a big job interview, on the way home after being fired, on the way to shooting your first day in the new *The Avengers* movie or on the way to your lawyer's office to sign divorce papers.

Where we're headed when we get that flat tire helps put our lives, and that particular challenge, into perspective. Each one is unique and timing is everything, and when it's *your* time, you'll know it.

However, you also have to be searching for the challenge and be aware of it when it comes. In other words, you have to be purposeful about looking for your passion.

That's why finding your passion usually precedes big life changes. Once you discover it, you can't wait to get started and that's how you know that it's time to launch your new life once and for all.

Don't get me wrong, it's very hard to lose everything you were raised to believe will make you happy and successful. Such a period of struggle may seem to be the worst time to change your life, when you barely have enough money to replace that flat tire, let alone start living the life you were meant to live.

Nonetheless, trust me. I had nothing when I was at my lowest and look at me now. I built my new life from the ground up, happily, even when challenges came one after another. When you're living your passion, it's easier to face difficulties because you know them for what they really are—life lessons and investments in your future.

Defining Moments Are Like Potato Chips: *You Can't Have Just One.*

Unfortunately, life is not like the movies. There was no director to yell "Cut!" that day in the doorway and the next scene didn't depict me running up some steps with *Rocky* music blaring in the background. It was a long, hard slog to where I am today, but I had to start somewhere.

Another thing I discovered is that once I had that first big, earth-shattering, foundation-clearing, defining moment, I started noticing them more and more often. I'd be walking somewhere, retreating to that dark place, thinking bad thoughts, feeling down on myself, trudging to another dead-end interview for another dead-end job and I'd see twelve other guys just like me on the subway platform and think, "*Stop it, Red! Stop rewriting the same old scene in the same old story. Scrap it, and write something new.*" It was like once I'd gotten a taste for something new, something better, I couldn't help but see opportunities more and more often, usually accompanied by many "mini" defining moments.

When will your defining moment come? There's no telling. It could hit you in the middle of the night, waking you out of a dead sleep. You could be driving home from your workplace, sitting in a movie theater or attending another dinner party and *BOOM!* Just like that, you'll get it. You'll think, this is *my* time to change!

Honestly, the sooner the better. If you're reading these words, if you've stuck with me this long, you're ready. I know you are. Who knows? Maybe *this* is your defining moment—reading these words, right now, right here.

I hope so because it's not healthy for us to be unhappy, to be low, to suffer from years of "going along to get along" without living our true passion. So let's get to it. Start living your life. Now.

CHAPTER 4

The Fourth Secret • Power • Knowing How to Get It

*"Only those who will risk going too far
can possibly find out how far one can go."*
T.S. Eliot (1888–1965), Twentieth-century poet

ower, for lack of a better term, is a very potent thing. With power we can do almost anything and without it we are more than just power-"less." We are useless to ourselves, to our friends and families, to our boss and our co-workers, to the planet.

There was a time in my life when I had no power and thus no direction. I had no energy, no control and no desire to gain control or take back the reins of my life. I felt that I was at the bottom and would always stay there.

After all, why not? As far as I could tell, I had no evidence to the contrary.

Before this low point, before I became powerless, I thought I knew what I wanted and I had a plan on how to get there. I was confident and sure of myself. I knew how the world worked, how to get around the system and how to win.

I never understood why others couldn't succeed, how they could be down, complaining about their circumstances and never know the secrets to getting ahead. "*What is wrong with them?*" I'd think as I sped by on my way to something and somewhere more important.

Losing Your Power.

Then something happened to me. One day, I discovered that I was in a place of not knowing and not having any control in my life. That sense of security, that power I'd had, vanished like steam from a cup of hot cocoa on a cold winter day.

It started simply enough. As you know from earlier passages, I found out that my marriage was unraveling. In fact, I would have done anything to make the relationship work.

That was what power was to me. Anything could be fixed, even if the other person didn't really want it to be put back together. All I could think was, "What did I do wrong and how can I fix it?"

No matter what I did, though, I couldn't fix my marriage. I had no control over the situation and it made me feel powerless. I felt like a puppet and someone else was pulling the strings. I felt lost and insecure about everything.

Perhaps you are in the same place in your life right now? Are you feeling out of control and want to take your control back? Would you like to get your mojo back at work or put the magic back in your relationship?

If you feel that someone else is making all the choices about what you experience and you're just along for the ride without the right to have a say, then you are like I was. When you're tired of feeling powerless, rudderless and out of control, you want nothing more than to get your power back.

Getting Your Power Back.

During my darkest days, when I felt as lost as I could possibly feel, I met a man named Bob. I had never before met anyone quite like him. He would ask me questions and it was like he was giving me answers without actually giving them to me. It was magical.

One day, when I was really down and out, he asked me, "Hey, Red, who has your power?" It was such a blunt but perfect question at the time. It was like he had peered into my soul and seen how powerless I felt. Or maybe he just got tired of watching me mope around everywhere.

Either way, I told him that I didn't have it anymore. "My power is gone," I confessed. Bob looked at me and asked again, "Red, *who* has your power?" Finally I said, "Someone took my power."

It was at that point that he taught me one of the most important lessons I've ever learned and that I apply to this day. "*No one* can take your power," he said. "You can only give it away."

It hit me like a sledgehammer at the time and the notion speaks to me more strongly every day since. So I'd like to repeat that for us both: "*No one* can take your power. You can only give it away."

Lesson 1: *No one and no thing can take your power. You can only give it away.*

Let this truth be your new mantra. Breathe it in, absorb it and live by it. *You and only you are in control of your life.* If you are succeeding and triumphing, that's on you. If you are failing miserably, well, that's on you too. Sometimes it feels easier for us to blame others for our successes and our failures, but the fact is that we're the architects of both.

When Bob further asked me, "Red, do you want to get your power back?" I blurted out "Of course. But I just don't know how to do it."

Sound familiar? Perhaps you are facing a similar situation right now. Maybe, no matter how hard you've tried, or for how long, you just don't know how to take back control of your life.

So what did Bob suggest to me that day? Well, in an unorthodox move (for me, anyway), he suggested that I attend a men's empowerment weekend. A men's empowerment weekend? "Hmm. I don't know, Bob. What does one do on a men's empowerment weekend?" "Just come, Red, and you'll find out."

So I did, and let me tell you, it was an eye opener. I am not generally what you would call a forthcoming man, at least I wasn't back then. Instead, I kept my feelings close to my vest, which quickly changed during that men's retreat.

Over the course of that weekend, I was stripped down and built up, from top to bottom, back and forth, over and over again. We started by taking a good, hard look at ourselves. Who were we? What did we stand for? What were we proud of and what were we afraid of?

Next we confronted ourselves by peeling away the layers of our personal onion. Layer by layer, we began the process of getting to our core—our passion and our truth—the pieces we had covered up for so long.

I faced parts of myself that I didn't want to face. My fears, obstacles, secrets, hopes, dreams, worries, anxieties and all of the other parts that were holding me back from living my life personally and powerfully. It took some time because the layers I'd built around myself—some protective, some delusional—took a while to strip away. We're all like that, I suppose.

Think of yourself as a nuclear reactor and the nuclear rod is your heart, your passion, and your power. And envision your heart encased in cooling water with a very thick concrete that surrounds and protects it.

Each of us has built these types of protective layers over the years. And since we've put them up ourselves, we also have the ability to peel away those layers, to pull them down and understand why we put them there in the first place. We must remove the heavy, seemingly intractable concrete and then the cooling water becomes the next obstacle, the moat that prevents us from reaching our core, where the beauty, energy, and power exists in all of us.

Lesson 2: *Start peeling your layers. To take back your mojo, you will need to take a look at yourself.*

If you want your power back, the second thing you need to do is quit lying to yourself. Be direct, be focused and, above all, strip away the protective layers you've built up over the years. So how do we do that?

You can join a support group like I did or you can ask your friends, colleagues or a coach for help. You can find a buddy, someone who can help you through the challenge of stripping away your layers, because it's very challenging to do this work by ourselves (more on teamwork and "the buddy system" in the next chapter).

But if we choose to do the work of taking our power back, we can start by asking ourselves the tough questions:

1) *Who or what did we give our power to?* Remember, no one can take your power. You can only give it away. So you need to work out just exactly who, or what, you are giving your power to.

2) *What are the obstacles we've placed in our way?* Before we can get back our power, we have to dig deeply to identify the self-placed obstacles in our way. These could be lies we tell ourselves, or a job we hate, or a situation we can't control or a house we no longer can live in or afford.

3) *List the obstacles.* Be specific and precise and, above all, honest. If one of your obstacles is an addiction, or a secret, or a crushing fear or even a phobia, admit it and write it down.

4) *List anything and everything that gets in your way.* Again, be precise. If you procrastinate, point this out to yourself—first by admitting it and then by listing it. Do this for every obstacle you face, big and small.

5) *Don't judge the list, just write down the obstacles.* None of us is perfect as we all have our foibles and fears. We needn't be afraid of what we reveal or be ashamed of it. Once you've written your list and admitted to the obstacles you've put in your path, you can begin to work on eradicating them.

The first step is knowing what's in our way. Then we can work on addressing each obstacle, one at a time, until each is removed and we can move forward to the next. Every obstacle we get rid of brings us closer to getting our power back.

At the core of this process is understanding ourselves better. To do this we have to strip down all the way to the core, layer by layer, and then build ourselves back up again. Don't worry about the time you'll spend as the more honest, open and realistic you are, the more powerful you'll be when you finally *do* get your mojo back. As I write this, I keep thinking about how often I would realize that, although I thought I had things figured out, I really had so much more to learn.

Once my marriage ended and I started dating again, I had a couple of lines that I fell back on when I would meet a woman. One of them went like this: "Don't fall in love with me, that's not what I'm looking for."

Now, it's not like every woman I met fell in love with me. In fact, there were many women that wouldn't even go out with me a second time. I was just being open and honest. I didn't want the women I was dating to get the wrong impression. My marriage had just ended and I had no intention of jumping into another relationship.

About eight months after my first wife and I separated, Phyllis (Phyl for short) and I went on our first date. We met for drinks at a chic downstairs bar on Forty-Fourth Street and Ninth Avenue.

Unfortunately, I had told her to meet me on *Fortieth* and Ninth instead of Forty-Fourth and Ninth. Not a good idea. Fortieth and Ninth is not a particularly savory little block, but there she was, standing there on a bad street corner, waiting for me just like I had asked.

Luckily, Phyl is a very good sport and just made a joke of it. Anyway, we ended up in the bar talking for hours and having a wonderful time—even after I used my "Don't fall in love me" line. I'm sure she thought, "You jerk. Why don't you try not falling in love with *me?*" Nonetheless, we had a great conversation, laughed a lot and I walked her home the thirty blocks from Forty-Fourth Street to Seventy-Sixth Street.

Something about Phyl interested me and we began seeing each other regularly (even though I was determined that I was not ready to get involved). Phyl had already been divorced for a few years and wanted a more serious relationship, but I did not, which meant that we entered into a "light switch" relationship.

It would be on for a while because I felt I was ready and then it would be off because I felt I wasn't. But even with my fluctuating mindset, when we were apart I felt this incredibly strong pull to be with her. Phyl felt the same way.

This torture went on for about a year and half. We would break up and then get back together again, depending on how I felt that particular moment. I thought, "Well, this is fine. Phyl will be there for me until I'm ready." Then one day Phyl decided that she wouldn't.

I remember sitting in her apartment as she told me that it wasn't working for her anymore. I couldn't believe it. I told her that if she wanted a break then it would be over and, to my astonishment, she said, "Fine." I left her apartment in a kind of daze, not really comprehending what had just happened. I felt like I had been hit by a bullet.

The next day I reached out to Phyl and asked her to reconsider, but it was to no avail as she felt very strongly about it. I had this huge void inside of me. How could we go from being together almost every day to not seeing each other at all? How could she do this to us? It was apparent to me that I'd ruined a relationship with a wonderful woman and that the opportunity may not arise again.

I remember asking God why He was doing this to me. What had I done to deserve all this pain and heartache? I asked Him to at least give me something to hold onto. Thankfully I still had my mom. She would listen to me bemoan my situation (almost every night) until I could fall asleep. I never forgot that lesson in love, I now do the same for my kids, friends, and family; I will make time for someone who's hurting for as long as he or she needs me.

My misery lasted about two months until I decided that it was time to pick up the pieces of my life once again. It was time to work on Red. The "Summer of Red" is what I called it. Besides, if I wasn't 100 percent, how could I be there for my kids? How could I ever be in a healthy relationship with a woman?

I went back to the gym and started visiting sick children in the hospital. I worked on my issues in my men's group and began to heal myself and become stronger. I felt my confidence returning and my life was beginning to improve.

A short time later, I bumped into Phyl on the street. I walked her about two blocks to her destination and asked her if the door to our relationship was even the slightest bit open. I was feeling in a much better place and felt sure that if it was open just a crack, that I could get her back in my life. She wouldn't answer me but, at that moment, I knew that I could bring her around. As we parted, I said, "One day I'm going to marry you."

The next few months passed quickly and I thoroughly enjoyed the Summer of Red. My friends Tehillah and Meryl opened their Fire Island houses to me and I spent many weekends there by the shore. It was a very chill and relaxing time. I was learning to live in the present, spending more and more time with my kids, my friends, and enjoying life.

On the Saturday before Labor Day, I was walking home from synagogue and I noticed Phyl walking ahead of me. I remember watching the bottom of her dress swaying with each of her steps. She was gorgeous.

Catching up to her before she could enter her apartment building and slip away from me, I asked, "Phyl... how are you?" After a brief moment of conversation, I then asked her if we could grab a drink, to which she responded, "To what end?"

"To catch up," I said. She said she'd think about it and would contact me to let me know. As we said goodbye, she gave me a light kiss on my lips and I knew that her answer would be yes.

We got together for drinks and we waited in line for New York's fabulous Shakespeare in the Park. We saw *Hair* and danced onstage at the performance. We began dating again and, three years later, we married each other…on Labor Day weekend.

My early relationship with Phyl taught me a few valuable lessons. I learned that until we understand ourselves it is very challenging to be in a healthy relationship. I also learned to live more lightly with the things I want and that we can attract what we'd like without grasping.

Finally, I learned that we often need to endure great pain to realize the beauty in our lives. That being a little less arrogant about the extent of my own insight was important. That sometimes, when we think we have it all figured out, we've really just scratched the surface of our understanding.

It took me a while to peel away the layers of my protective ego and to see that my greatest happiness lied in sharing my life with Phyl. By having the courage to really understand who you are and the obstacles you've created to your greatest happiness, you can emerge as a person of *real* confidence and power. Then you can go about the important work we've started here, discovering the reasons you were put on this planet.

No More Trying: *Taking Your Power Back, One Word at a Time.*

Before you can get your power back, you have to believe that you can actually achieve your goal. Before you can shake whatever's been sapping you, dragging you down or holding you back, you must first believe that you have the power to make it happen. This starts with the words you use.

It may sound corny, but words have power and the more you *hear* them, the more power they have. Believe me, I've attempted to succeed without using words that empower me, but you simply can't get your power back if you don't believe that you can.

Some words have more power than others. For instance, the words "I can do it" are uplifting and can take you to new heights and new places. That's because they feed your power rather than sap it.

In contrast, other words can take away your power even though they are disguised as powerful. Take the word "try" for instance. Try is just another excuse for failure. In my experience, the more we "try" the less we actually do.

Trying feels like doing, but it's a lot like treading water: You can flail your arms and kick your legs and get your heart rate up and even sweat a little but, in the end, you simply don't go anywhere.

Think of the ways we typically use the word "try" and how quickly, and obviously, it becomes an excuse. I *tried* to take out the garbage. I *tried* to pay that bill before the due date. I *tried* to show up for that job interview on time. I *tried* to call you.

You *tried* to call me? How did you *try* to call me? Was the phone too heavy? Were there too many digits to dial? How could you *not* make that happen? Either you called me, or you didn't.

The fact is, "try" is one big excuse and we know it. So do the people we say it to. So, in your effort to take back your power, start with this one simple word. Instead of saying you "tried" to do something, say what you really meant. You *chose* not to do something.

I *chose* not to take out the garbage. I *chose* not to pay that bill before the due date. I *chose* not to show up for that job interview on time. I *chose* not to call you.

When we're honest with ourselves we can see where our power is being sapped. If we're not getting what we want, we can either attempt to make ourselves feel better by saying we "tried" or we can be honest and say we chose not to do something. The more honest we are, the more we can see that we didn't really try at all, allowing us to move forward with integrity.

For years, I *tried* to write this book until I realized that trying was just another way of saying I was choosing not to write it. So I didn't *try* to write this book. I *am* writing it. I didn't *try* to finish this chapter. I *am* finishing it.

And you know what? It wasn't as hard as I thought it would be. The fact is that nothing ever is. So, no more trying. From now on, there is only doing. Let today be the day you erase "try" from your vocabulary.

Word Power: *An Activity for You.*

For this chapter, I really wanted to provide you with an exercise that would support my feelings about word power and show you how influential words are not just to our emotions, but also to our physical actions.

So, to close the chapter on getting your power back, I'm going to provide you with one question to help you achieve that goal and one tool to make it real. The question is: *Do you listen to the words you use when you speak?*

I know you hear them, but do you actually *listen* to them? Are you conscious of your choice of words and do you take them in or do you just keep saying the same things over and over again as if no one's really listening? If it is the second option that is the case, no one *will* listen because they've heard it all before.

Now, to the tool I promised you. It is simple, yet effective. *Become more conscious of the words you choose to use.*

Words are powerful. They are, quite literally, more than just words. They don't just affect us emotionally, but they affect us physically as well. They impact our decisions, our relationships, our jobs, our marriages, our successes and our failures. The words we use, whether consciously or subconsciously, make up who we are and how we act. We can use them to weaken us or we can use them to empower us and make us stronger.

In the past, I used many negative words. They would drag me down and push me away from my passion. I felt as if I couldn't accomplish anything, as if I were numb, as if I were dying my life rather than living it. That is the power of negative words—they can destroy us, but only if we let them. So what are some negative words?

Can't. "I can't do it. I just can't do it. I can't take it anymore." Or the word *never.* Yes, believe it or not, the word "never" is a negative word. "I'm never late," or "I never do that." Or the phrase, *I'm hanging in there.* "Hey, Joe, how you doing?" "I'm hanging in there." "Okay, good." Negative, negative, negative.

Remember what I said earlier. No one can take your power, you can only give it away. So to say that someone *made* you mad, or sad or even glad isn't being quite truthful. What you mean when you say that someone "made you feel a certain way" is that you *allowed* someone to make you feel a certain way.

I'll try a little exercise with you. Wherever you are right now, I want you do to me a favor. Call me ugly. Just shout it out. I may not be able to hear you, but I'll feel you say it. Just say, "Red, you're ugly."

And say it like you mean it. Say it as if you want to hurt my feelings. Bring it up from your diaphragm, and let me hear it all the way from Albuquerque or Miami or Fresno or Honolulu. Ready? On the count of three. One, two, three. "Red, you're ugly!"

Here's my answer to you, "I don't care." I never was ugly and I don't have any ugly issues. Sure, I'm not Clark Gable or Brad Pitt, but how many of us look like those guys? While I'm no movie star, I still don't care as I was never insecure about that part of myself.

On the flip side, when I was younger and my hairline began receding (or shall I be politically correct and say I became follically challenged?), if someone made a comment about it, I would feel bad and want to hide.

As time passed and I realized that women loved running their fingers through my thick, luxurious…scalp, I didn't care about the comments anymore. People still made them and the same words were used either in humor or sarcasm, but the difference was how I *felt* about myself then and how I feel now.

No one *made* me feel anything with their words. I felt differently because I changed how I felt about *myself.*

Just as no one can make you feel negative, and no one can diminish your passion. We can use words that set ourselves up to fail and lose faith in ourselves or we can use words that set ourselves up to succeed and build on our own strengths. I choose the latter. I hope you do too.

Are You Hanging or Swinging?

I'll ask my friends how they're doing and their response is usually something like, "I'm hanging in there, Red." Whenever they say that, I picture them stuck in place, just hanging there like a stick figure in a real-life game of hangman.

You know what I say when someone asks me how I'm doing? Go ahead. Ask me. "Red, how ya doin'?" My answer? "I'm swinging, baby. I am swinging!"

It's true because life is a lot like a swing, going back and forth and up and down. My life may not be going so well at the moment. I may have lost my job or gotten a divorce, or I may need an operation or a loan, so I may be swinging backward. Just picture this: The more pain I am in, the more I may be swinging back in my life, the more momentum I'll have when I swing forward.

A few months ago I may have been in a low spot but suddenly, on the upswing, I might have found a new job, gotten a raise or even regained my health. My life may not be perfect yet, I may still need a new transmission in my car or a washing machine in my house, but my momentum is going forward and so I'm still swinging.

Life is like that, I've discovered. You swing forward a little, you swing back a lot. You swing forward a lot, you swing back a little. Either way, you're moving. Sadly, some people I know are just hanging. Hanging around, hanging onto despair or literally hanging in one place, dying their life instead of living it.

So are you hanging or swinging? Either way, you have the power to decide. And that power lies within your words and how you choose to frame the events that happen to you. Words are powerful as they become thoughts and thoughts become actions.

Negative words lead to negative thoughts which lead to negative actions. Positive words lead to positive thoughts which lead to positive actions. Remember, the choice is yours.

CHAPTER 5

The Fifth Secret • Teamwork • The Buddy System

"Alone we can do so little; together we can do so much."
**Helen Keller (1880–1968), American humanitarian
and advocate for the deaf and blind**

L et's face it, sometimes we all need a helping hand. Sometimes the task of finding our power is too much work for us to do alone. Even our passion itself can require a friend, or a team of friends, to bring it to life at times.

Bill Gates may be the face of Microsoft, but he couldn't bring his passion to life all by himself. Stephen Spielberg might be the name most associated with *Jaws*, but he was never alone on the set.

The importance of being willing to rely on others became apparent to me years ago when I found my business unraveling. It was the summer of 1998 and at the same time that I was on the beach with my ex-wife and kids, I was also on the phone with my attorney, working on closing a deal to buy another accessory company.

I knew how to streamline companies and make them work more efficiently by cutting out the fat and outsourcing many of the mundane tasks. I thought this purchase was going to help me do that—as well as increase sales and profits.

One of my bankers didn't like the deal and kept telling me that it was too risky. I thought that he was just a pessimist. *He was a banker, not a risk taker*, I told myself. There was no way he was going to deter me from completing my acquisition and building my company.

After all, I had created my company from nothing. I was smarter than he was and I could make anything work. I felt great after I got off the phone. We had wrapped up the final details of the acquisition and we were set to close that week.

A brief time later I moved into my new office space, a full floor on Fifth Avenue and Thirty-Eighth Street. I had about fifty people working for me and I, of course, had the corner office. I was on top of the world. The euphoria lasted about a month.

While I thought I had purchased a company that would propel my business's growth, I had actually bought the Titanic—and it had already hit the iceberg. The new company's open order report was not what it seemed as some of the orders didn't exist and others were not profitable. And there were no additional orders in the pipeline. I thought that I'd done my due diligence, but my "ultimate optimist" attitude deterred me from looking carefully at the state of the company I was buying. Now I was paying the price.

I remember sitting in my apartment at the dining room table six weeks after the purchase and realizing that my new company's accounts payable was a good deal more than I originally projected. I had to make a huge payroll every week and there was not enough money coming in to cover it, the bills and the payments for the new company.

I felt alone and desperate as I realized that I had made a *huge* mistake. My banker had been right; this was not a good deal. I had no one to turn to. I had no support system. I had created all this on my own.

I had to keep borrowing money from my bank to keep afloat and, two weeks later, my banker asked me into his office. The CEO, my banker and two other bank representatives sat on one side of the table and I sat alone on the other. It felt surreal.

They wanted to cut my borrowing line and were not going to keep funding my new acquisition. I couldn't breathe. In two months, I had gone from being on top of the world to facing financial ruin.

After that meeting, I realized that I needed to close down the new company. Fortunately, I'd been smart enough to incorporate it as its own entity so I could keep my old business separate from the new company's debt, but I was scared.

I was receiving daily calls from creditors and I was afraid to let any collectors into our office. I was negotiating the payout with the former owner's attorneys and delaying the payments on my own personal bills. I didn't know how I could continue to afford paying for private school for our three children, our apartment in a Manhattan luxury high-rise and all the other expenses we had.

And then the other shoe dropped. I couldn't fathom how it could get worse, but it did. My wife got sick with an illness that left her unable to even go outside by herself. We began to go see a slew of doctors, but none of them could diagnose what was wrong. I had to physically carry her into cabs and then from the cabs to the doctors' offices.

So there I was…struggling to save my company from financial ruin, missing days at the office taking my wife to doctor appointments and taking care of our seven, five and three-year-old children. I recall one night, when my wife was feeling particularly bad, I begged her to get well so we could survive it as a team. I felt that with her by my side I could pull it all together. But I couldn't do it alone.

I desperately needed help, so I reached out to my parents. They are wonderful people and would do anything for their children or grandchildren. All they asked was how they could help. They offered to come to our apartment and help take care of my family so I could keep my business afloat. And a few hours later, they were at my door.

That image will forever be embedded in my memory. My mom was carrying her overnight bag and my dad was holding his classic black and silver Samsonite luggage. I was overwhelmed with emotion. Just seeing them, I felt a huge weight lifted off my shoulders. I didn't have to do this alone. My mom went straight to our kids and began to take care of them. She did their homework with them, bathed them, fed them and put them to bed. She would take them to school and pick them up—day in and day out.

My wife's mother also came and helped by taking her to her doctor's appointments. She stayed home with her during the day to care for her so I could go back to the office. And that's where my dad stepped in as he actually accompanied me to work to offer moral support.

I remember one day I had to lay off many of my employees. I would ask them into my office, one at a time, and explain the situation to them. It was a terrible experience and, as the day progressed, I turned to my dad and told him I couldn't do another thing.

Since I wasn't really accomplishing anything, he suggested that we leave the office and take a walk. My office was near the Forty-Second Street library and Bryant Park, so we sat on a park bench, just the two of us, and I told him that I couldn't handle the pressure anymore. It was too much.

As my world was collapsing around me, he took my hand in his hand and just held it. I felt his large, warm fingers over mine and all of a sudden I was his little boy again. He was my superman who could protect me from the world, letting nothing harm me.

I was so overwhelmed that I put my head on his shoulder and started to cry. It was the middle of a bright, sunny day and there we were—two men sitting on a bench in Bryant Park, holding hands and crying.

During that time, I learned that I didn't have to do it alone. I could ask for support and love. My parents weren't wealthy and they couldn't help us financially, but what they offered my family and I was so much more valuable than money. They showed up and inspired me to get up each morning and solve my financial problems. Their unconditional love and support gave me the strength and resolve to fix my own mess.

My dad was able to stay with us for a couple of weeks and my mom and mother-in-law stayed many more helping with my kids and my wife. I was able to negotiate a settlement with the attorneys of the recently purchased company and was even able to salvage my old firm.

After I closed down the new company, the business moved back to the old building on Thirty-Third Street and my wife's health was restored. It was a complete circle within twelve months and I learned that, even as a full-fledged adult, it was perfectly okay to allow those who were willing to, to step in and help me manage a difficult time. Sometimes we all need a helping hand, which is why this chapter is called "The Buddy System."

Without someone consciously rooting for us and someone to hold us accountable, we often lose our momentum as we move into a new way of living. It can feel overwhelming and quite foreign and, at times, we're likely to find ourselves asking how we continue living our passion every day. How do we focus on the things we want and yet manage the tasks of our daily lives? How do we keep our momentum?

Before we know it, time has passed and another week has flown by, or a month, a year, a few years or a decade. Still, after all that time, we're not any closer to living our passion.

Many times I've read a book just like this or gone to a seminar or listened to an audiobook and gotten revved up, energized and ready to rebuild or restart my life, only to wake up the next morning, grumble "meh" and roll over and go right back to sleep.

It's easy to lose traction. I've seen countless people (myself included) cling to horribly unsatisfying, even dysfunctional circumstances because somehow there is comfort in the known. But this is not a program about staying stuck and this is not a book about finding excuses. It's a book about finding your passion.

Let me share with you one of the most important tools for finding and then living your passion. It continues to work for me to this very day and I call it "The Buddy System." (No, the phrase is not original, but it's still very apropos, so stick with me here.)

Remember when you were in kindergarten? That was the golden age of the buddy system. We always had our buddies around, from the time we got to school until the final bell of the day.

At the beginning of the year, the teacher would tell everyone to choose a buddy and we normally picked our friends. I would have loved to pick a cute girl, but I went to an all-boys school so that wasn't happening. Instead, I picked my best friend.

We'd choose our buddy for the class trips too. On the bus, the teacher would say, "Buddies, hold hands." Once we got off the bus, the teacher would say, "Buddies, stay together" or "Watch out for your buddy" or "Keep your buddy in sight" and on and on.

These buddies held us accountable. We were responsible for each other. We took care of each other. We loved each other.

Yes, the book by Robert Fulghum, *All I Really Needed to Know I Learned in Kindergarten* (1986), is as accurate these days as ever. What we learn in kindergarten can guide us through our entire lives. If we follow the same principles from way back then, starting with the buddy system, we will get where we need to be. Okay, so we all know how well the buddy system works as kids, but it's hardly repeatable as adults, right? Wrong.

Sure, it may look a little different as grown-ups—I don't necessarily need to hold my buddy's hand, although I did hold my dad's in the park and, at the time, it was pretty comforting—but the principles still hold true in adult life.

Respect one another. Look out for each other. Bounce things off one another. Support one another. Watch your buddy's back. Argue with one another. Love each other.

Let's see how the buddy system might work for you today. Start by thinking about the people in your life that you can count on. Now ask yourself, "Of the people I know in my heart that would be there for me, and I for them, who would make the best buddy?" My suggestion?

Don't choose your significant other. This is not a particularly wise choice for your buddy because you already share so much with him or her. Plus, your buddy should not be someone who will be intimately affected by your life changes.

Don't choose either of your parents or a sibling either. They bring too much baggage with the family relationship and may be disinclined to invest fully in your passion. So who would make a good buddy?

Just like in kindergarten, a good friend can make a very worthy buddy. As long as that person is someone you can trust and rely on. Someone who loves you and whom you love back in every sense of your friendship.

When choosing your friend though, be sure to pick someone who's not afraid to play devil's advocate or, when it's called for, be a goading cheerleader. Choose someone who "gets" you, who is easy to talk to, who doesn't mind brainstorming, or spitballing, or calling you out when you're full of yourself.

A buddy isn't a "yes" person. He or she is someone who will support you, yes, but also who isn't afraid to pull at the threads of some harebrained scheme if it sounds full of holes and needs to be tightened up a bit before going live. A good buddy can help you see yourself more clearly while still supporting you and cheering you on toward your ultimate goal. Why do you need a buddy?

Accountability. It's just that simple. What do I mean by that? Well, first, let me explain how passion works. In trying to find our passion, many of us fail because we simply lose momentum. We let ourselves slide too easily and we lose ourselves rather quickly.

When we don't hold ourselves accountable—and accountability is at the heart of the buddy system—we make promises that we don't keep. Promises such as, I'll start that diet…*tomorrow*. I'll work on my resume…*next week*. I'll start jogging…*next month*.

Then, suddenly, it is six months later and we're still in the same place. This is not my opinion. This is data. This is fact. Want to know how I know? Just look at the fitness industry.

How do gyms make millions of dollars? Simple. They make fortunes on people who don't follow through, who don't have a buddy to keep them accountable and who joined a gym only because of some dumb resolution.

Case in point: Gym memberships skyrocket in January. Why? New Year's resolutions. They offer "special" deals in January knowing full well that it's a profitable setup for them with little expenditure of time or resources for your fat fee (both literally and figuratively).

They get you in, sign you up for a full year's commitment, take your down payment and, after a few months—sometimes even a few weeks—they stop seeing you come through the door even though they'll see your money for the rest of the year! They are salivating for your payments and know they're going to get them because of the way the human mind works.

It's like shooting fish in a barrel. January's here, you sign up, suddenly you're going to the gym twice a week and you're feeling super. "This is sooo easy," you say to yourself. "I feel amazing!"

Then February rolls around. Hmm, not so easy anymore. You're busy, you're not seeing the kind of results you saw at first and your motivation is failing. It's harder and harder to find time to make it to the gym so now instead of going twice a week, you're going once a week, if that.

Then March rolls around. It's been ages since you've gone to the gym, but you feel extremely motivated one morning and are ready to go until you realize that, oh wow, you've lost your membership card. "Well, I can't go now," you think and flop back onto the couch. (Never mind the fact that you could probably get a replacement at the front desk on your way in the door.) Soon April comes along and by now you're asking, "What gym did I belong to again?"

Hmm, sound familiar? Is this you? If it is, please don't worry. This is the no-judgment zone. We've all been there. In fact, if this does sound like you, then know that you're actually in the majority. Most people fail at their New Year's resolutions, particularly when it comes to health, fitness, weight loss...and gym attendance. Why?

Lack of accountability. It can be very, very hard to keep ourselves accountable when excuses crop up or life gets in the way. However, if we have a buddy that can make all the difference because buddies hold us accountable.

We don't want to lose face with our friends. We don't want to listen to them question us or our work ethic. We also don't want them to question our commitment to ourselves and, most importantly, we don't want them to question our commitment to them. But have we? Have we made a commitment to them? Yes. Yes, we have. That's what buddies do.

Now imagine the same New Year's resolution scenario, but this time you're using the buddy system. Now when March hits, instead of making an excuse to ourselves, we've got to inform our buddy about our progress.

"You going to the gym today?" our buddy might ask. "No," we'll answer. "Why not?" they ask. "Lost my membership card," we respond. "That's a lame excuse," they say. "They'll give you a replacement at the front desk. Come on. I'll meet you there in ten." *BOOM!* Excuse deflated, commitment reignited.

I'm not saying that having a buddy to hold our feet to the fire will work every time, but it often gives impetus to our individual pursuits. As for me, I want to be a man of my word, a man of integrity. I want people to know that

I will do what I say I will do and be a man on whom they can count. I live up to my commitments and keep my word. I'll also follow through on my resolution, so I don't have to deal with the feedback. Hence, the *buddy* system.

Twenty Minutes and the Buddy System.

A great way to keep yourself on task is to commit to your buddy that you'll work toward your goal twenty minutes each week. Please don't tell me that you don't have twenty minutes during the course of seven whole days to live your passion as we can all set aside twenty minutes if we want to.

For instance, have you always wanted to write a book but never found the time? If you have, then I'm guessing that you've been thinking about that book for years but was just too daunted to ever begin. However, in bite-sized chunks, even the Great American Novel becomes manageable.

So commit to your buddy that you'll work toward that goal for twenty minutes every week and have them help you stick to it. After a while you'll start to feel good about yourself and, eventually, it'll be twenty minutes twice a week. Then you'll feel more ambitious and you'll add a few minutes of writing each time and it will be thirty minutes twice a week, or forty minutes three times a week and so on. In fact, before you know it, you'll have finished your book – just like I have!

Our buddies help us along our path, looking out for us, protecting us, supporting us and making sure that we stick to our weekly quota. And they'll be there to lend a helping hand when needed. Our buddies will help us with all of our other passions and we'll start to help out our buddies too. We hold each other accountable.

Don't look at the end goal because it may overwhelm you and you'll think it's unachievable. After all, how can you possibly write a book with just twenty minutes each week, right? Easy. Just take that first step.

Think about the first passion you want to touch on, the one you've been holding back from pursing, the one that's screaming the loudest because it wants to be heard. Don't wait any longer. Line up a buddy to serve as your support and your taskmaster and then commit to twenty minutes a week. Give your passion a voice and do something about it.

Not tomorrow. Not next week. Not next month. Not next year. Give your passion a voice *now*. Your passion, and you, deserve to be heard.

CHAPTER 6

The Sixth Secret • Initiative • Knowing How to Get Started

"The fishermen know that the sea is dangerous and the storm terrible,
but they have never found these dangers sufficient reason
for remaining ashore."
Vincent van Gogh (1853–1890),
Dutch painter and former art salesman

So now we're really getting to the heart of the matter, aren't we? I mean, finding your passion is one thing, but going out and living it? Taking risks? Making changes? Switching jobs? Quitting jobs? Going back to school? Putting your feet to the pavement and making real progress toward living your YOUlogy? That takes some work.

I can remember sitting there, bottom of the barrel, no money in my pockets, living in my brother's basement, lower than low and filling my head with excuses as to why I couldn't make the leap to becoming a public speaker. That was my passion. I'd figured it out. I wanted it more than anything, but I simply couldn't do what I needed to do to make it reality. I wanted it, and I wanted it right then.

I couldn't see the journey to my first speaking gig, but I could easily picture the gig itself. I envisioned the adulation, the crowd, the applause, the laughter and the tears. I could picture the faces of the people in the audience, feel their appreciation for inspiring them to change their lives and feel the satisfaction of knowing I'd done something good for total strangers.

I could taste it, smell it and feel it, but I just couldn't get up off the couch to do a single thing about it. I tried and tried and tried again, and we all know how impactful that activity was, right? But I had plenty of other excuses, too.

I had no money. I had no time. I had no energy. I had no contacts. I had no resources. I had no "ins" or connections. But then one day it hit me. I didn't have to do it all at once. I'd been doing pretty much nothing for months at that point, so if all I did was one extra thing a day, I'd at least be doing something. I'd at least be moving forward. I'd at least be working toward something, working toward my passion.

One Step a Day.

Getting your power back, finding your voice and going after your passion doesn't happen in a day. And waking up and waiting for inspiration to strike doesn't work either. Inspiration doesn't strike; it hums all day long, like background noise. If you choose to listen to it, if you prick up your ears and focus on it, you can hear it quite clearly as it quickly becomes foreground noise.

Realistically mammoth goals aren't achieved overnight. For example, if you're a coach potato then you can't just Netflix *Chariots of Fire* on Friday night and expect to run a marathon on Saturday morning. Life doesn't work that way. In fact, if you were to attempt to run a marathon with absolutely no training, you'll be out of breath and cramping up after only a mile or two.

On the other hand, if you wake up on Saturday morning with a simple five-minute baby-step goal, you *can* create a positive experience that will propel you toward spending another five minutes—maybe the next day, maybe later in the week—and another five and another five.

So maybe that first Saturday you dust off your old running shoes, stretch and take a brisk walk around the block. It feels good, so you make it a goal to walk for five minutes three times every week. Once you're used to that and loving it, you bump up the duration and choose to walk for ten minutes three times a week, then fifteen minutes four times, and so on. Maybe you even start jogging every other day or for half the time you're out on the trail.

Then, after a few months or even a few years later, you have worked up to running a 5K run for charity in your town and maybe after that a full-blown marathon. That's how motivation works, that's how we create our passion and that's how we make things stick, *really* stick.

To get your power back once and for all, you have to make working on your passion a daily habit. That's why I suggest small increments of five, ten, fifteen and twenty minutes.

Look at it another way. There are 1,860 steps in the Empire State Building and let's say that one of your goals is to walk up to the top. Well, most mere mortals can't climb 1,860 steps in one day as that's a marathon in itself. However, if you climb one step a day, you can reach the top of the Empire State Building in five short years.

I say "short" years because, let's face it, five years is really not a long time. Think of your life in five-year increments. That's college, or the time it takes before your child goes into kindergarten, or the years you spent in your new house or on the new job. They fly by.

Remember, swing, don't hang. As long as you're moving forward, the momentum will keep you moving. Some days you may take two steps forward, other days you may take a step or two backward. But guess what? You're still making progress if you…Just. Keep. Moving.

That's how we find our passion, reach our goals and take our power back. One day, one minute, one goal, one accomplishment and one step at a time. Still, you have to be willing to take the first step and that's what this book is all about.

Life Is a Journey, Not a Destination.

What I learned by seeking out my passion is that life doesn't stop once you've reached your goals. That's actually a good thing. If we're lucky, life goes on and on and on and on. For the majority of us, however, a side effect of creating our passion is doubt and feeling anxious and scared.

You don't just get to the top and stay there without feeling anything before, during or after your trek. Life is a journey, not a destination. We feel joy, we feel pain. We win, we lose. We live, we die. Our friends live and die, and then more friends die. Our bank accounts are in the black, then the red, then the black again.

The only constant about life is that we're breathing. Everything else is up for grabs. So I still get low and doubtful and, occasionally, even have feelings of despair. And when I find myself in these mental, physical or spiritual slumps, I remember what got me to my passion in the first place—baby steps.

Even now that I'm back on track, enjoying my dream life as a speaker, author, husband and father, I still have days when I feel a bit overwhelmed by my commitments and my to-do list. On those days, I revisit this model and just focus on doing one thing at a time.

So, you're here, you're reading this book and you're wondering how to begin. As I said before, start something, anything. I can't read your mind and I don't know your passion but, as an example, let's say you'd love to do pottery. That's a great passion. But how do you get started in it if you've never touched clay in your life, let alone design a pot, vase, ashtray or coffee cup?

Well, first off, you don't let your lack of knowledge stop you. People who don't live their passions are stuck not because they don't know what they want to do, but because they just don't know how to get started.

So, pottery. How do you get started then? I actually have no idea. So here's where I'd start, if that were *my* passion. I'd buy a book. It doesn't have to cost much, so I would probably go on eBay and sniff around or buy a used one on Amazon and have it shipped to me.

With it I might learn what it would take to not only make pottery but also how to make a living out of it. If that interests me, I would read more books and if I can't afford too many, I would go to the library, visit websites or watch YouTube tutorials. (You can find out how to do almost anything, and I do mean *anything*, on YouTube these days.)

Do. Something. Start. Something. It's not just pottery I'm talking about. We all need to start somewhere. Whether you're into plants, or want to start a nursery, or go to medical school, or play professional baseball, or start a kids' league, or have a souvenir stand selling signed baseballs, do something. Start somewhere.

If you can do one thing, you can do two things. If you can buy one book on pottery, you can find something in that book to do the next day and the next and the next. Maybe will find a local art store to purchase clay. You don't even have to go in and get the clay yet, just find the store. That's something.

Maybe pottery is expensive, so you take a part-time job at an art school where pottery is a part of the curriculum. Now you're learning while you earn. And maybe you meet someone there who's in a pottery club that you can join, which you do and now you go there three times a week. That's something. That's several somethings.

There Are No Shortcuts: *Or, Don't Forget the Tortoise and the Hare.*

Remember the tortoise and the hare? Talk about baby steps. Who would ever believe a turtle could win a race against a rabbit? Nonetheless he did, but only because he signed up for the race in the first place. Once at the starting line, the tortoise committed to winning, one step at a time. He didn't sprint. He *couldn't* sprint. It's as impossible for a tortoise to sprint as it is for me to climb all 1,860 stairs to the top of the Empire State Building in one day.

However, the tortoise kept at it, day after day, step after step, footstep after footstep. He didn't focus on what he didn't have. He focused on what he *did* have. What did he have? Iron lungs, steely determination, and four feet.

And he walked those four feet across the finish line ahead of the hare because the hare did not have commitment.

The hare thought he could stop, rest, flit around and socialize, and just take the tortoise for granted, but the tortoise surprised him. You can surprise yourself too, if only you'll get started using baby steps one day at a time, day after day, week after week.

Imagine how the tortoise must have felt, inches away from the finish line with the hare nowhere in sight, knowing he was going to win and looking back on just how far he'd come. It was a slow process and he could never be sure the hare would stop for naps, or breaks, or other sundry and assorted activities. Instead, he could be sure of one thing. He won that race with all his heart, without cheating or shortcuts, and his path was there behind him to prove it.

Think of where you could be this time next week, next month or even next year if you were to simply start today by putting one foot in front of the next. Could you have that Master's degree you've always wanted to get? Open that business you've always wanted to start? Learn to play guitar and join a band? Get that promotion? Get your real estate license? Learn to scuba dive? Write that novel or screenplay (or book)?

The fact is that you'll never know unless you try. Scratch that, reverse it, rewind. We're not trying anymore, remember? We're doing. So I'll amend that statement. You'll never know until you *do*. Just. Do. Something.

It's how the tortoise got started, and look how far he got.

CHAPTER 7

A Bonus Secret • *Confidence* • *Knowing Your Worth*

"They can because they think they can."
Virgil (70 BC–19 BC), Roman poet

Confidence is a gift we give ourselves. This sounds like a bumper sticker, I know, but take it from a guy who had zero confidence as recently as a few short years ago. It's true. Just as no one can take our power, only we can give ourselves the confidence we need to find, and live, our passion. Only we can be confident enough to live our own YOUlogy, but we can't just tell ourselves to be more confident. We must actually feel our confidence inside ourselves.

Lack of confidence is basically insecurity and I believe that a great many people live their lives in a state of insecurity—without the benefit of knowing how blessed they are. Because really, what is a lack of confidence if not a lack of belief in your blessings?

When we know our true value, when we know how blessed we are, how unlike anyone else on the planet we are and how good we truly have it, then I believe we will have the power to not just find our passion, but to know that the possibilities for us are endless. But first, you must believe you are blessed.

You Are Blessed.

Life is good. It may not seem like it as you read this, because maybe you're depressed, or broke, or sad, or recently divorced, or a permanent bachelor or bachelorette. Or, perhaps you're a depressed, broke, sad, recently divorced guy living in his brother's basement. Maybe that's you and, if it is, that's okay because you know what? You're still blessed!

Stay with me here. Life is good and I know this for myself because I get up in the morning so, by default, I'm already ahead of the game. I wake up and I have complete use of all my limbs. I'm in a warm bed with a roof over my head. I go to the bathroom all by myself. I have food on the table—maybe a little, maybe a lot—but I have food. I get to speak to people for a living and help them find their passion. My family is healthy. And I live in one of the most exciting cities in the world.

So already, waking up in my own bed with a roof over my head, friends and family around, my health and living in New York City (no offense to the rest of the country), I'm already ahead of 99 percent of the nation before breakfast. Plus, the more I think about what I do have, the less I focus on what I don't have.

Life is good. Correction. Life is *great*.

I can say that now. I couldn't always say it. Furthermore, I say this as someone who lived through depression—a deep depression with suicidal thoughts—at rock bottom. So how can anyone who lives through a depression like that think life is not just good, but that it's great?

Through that time period, I learned the fundamental difference between what I *want* and what I *need*. Once upon a time I thought, "I need to make X amount of money. How can I be happy with anything less?" I also thought, "I need to live in a high-rise apartment on the Upper West Side. How can I be happy with anything less?" I'm not even done yet.

"I need a housekeeper to clean my penthouse apartment. How can I be happy with anything less?" Nope. I'm still not done. "My kids need to go to private school. How can they get a good education with anything less?"

Maybe it's human nature to gravitate to what we don't have, to dwell on that which eludes us, to obsess over what others have that we don't. However, I learned through rebuilding my life and writing my own YOUlogy that the difference between want and need isn't how much money we make, but how satisfied we are with ourselves.

I'm a happy guy and that is even though there are a lot of things I still want to have in my life. So why am I so happy? Because I have so much more than I *need*. I realized how blessed I was when I seemed to have the fewest blessings of all. Does that make sense?

Once I was stripped of all the bells and whistles, once I had lost all I wanted, needed, and everything in between, once I'd hit rock bottom and felt as though I had nothing left, I stopped myself from plunging even deeper into depression by beginning to focus on what I *did* have.

When my hours were the bleakest and my thoughts the darkest, I took heart in the old Rosemary Clooney song, *Count Your Blessings*, and counted my blessings instead of sheep. In my darkest hours, here's what got me through:

MY THREE BEAUTIFUL CHILDREN, MICHAELA, ARIEL, AND ZOE.

They're gorgeous, they're kind, they're generous and thoughtful—and they stuck by me when things got roughest. I couldn't have made it without them.

But maybe you don't have children. Don't we need children to be happy? Don't we need children to complete us? Nope. We could have siblings.

I HAVE THREE WONDERFUL BROTHERS, SAM, YONI AND DAVID.

Yes, there are four of us on this planet. There was a time when I spent the night in a place that wasn't the most pleasant and my brothers wanted to help me so much, but they just couldn't. When Yoni learned of this, he slept on the floor in solidarity. He knew I wasn't sleeping in a comfortable place, so he didn't want to either. How can you not feel blessed with brothers like that?

If we have no children and no siblings, don't we have a right to be miserable? We need one of those to feel happy and blessed, don't we?

Nope, we could have wonderful parents.

I HAVE INCREDIBLE PARENTS—ROBERT AND MIRIAM KATZ.

Loving, giving, kind and unconditional in their love, my parents have always been one of my biggest blessings, even when I felt ashamed to admit just how far I'd fallen.

Just look. They can boogie down. It's never too late to touch your passion.

Perhaps we don't have parents. No children, no siblings and no parents. We definitely have a right to be miserable, don't we?

Nope, we could have a life partner.

THIS IS MY WONDERFUL, BEAUTIFUL, GENEROUS
AND LOVING WIFE, PHYLLIS.

She came along when I needed her most and stuck around even when times were very tough. She is such a wonderful blessing. Thank God she stayed.

What if we don't have a life partner? We definitely need a partner to be happy, don't we? What if we have no parents, no children, no siblings and no life partner? We definitely have a right to be miserable then. We have no blessings. We have nothing, right?

Nope, we could have old friends.

TWO OF MY BEST AND OLDEST FRIENDS ARE YINGY AND ELLIOT.

I've known Yingy since seventh grade and I've known Elliot since college. These two friends have been my rocks through the good times and bad. No matter what happens, I want these two buddies in my foxhole. By the way, this is why they call me "*Red.*"

Let's say we don't have any friends. We really have nothing in our lives. We are miserable and we have every right to be. We have no blessings and we have every right to complain all day long, don't we?

Nope. We can make new friends.

I LIVE IN NEW YORK CITY.

All I need to do is walk outside and I can meet new people every day and make new friends. When my life gets in a rut, or at least feels that way, I can walk just a few blocks and suddenly I'm reminded that I live in one of the greatest cities on the planet. How's that for a blessing?

So let's say you don't live in New York City. Let's say you live in a very small town that has a population of only five hundred. You've met everyone and don't have any friends.

Let's sum it up, shall we? No children, no siblings, no parents, no partner, no friends and no possibility to make new friends. Okay, you win. You have a right to complain because your life is terrible, right?

NOPE. YOU STILL HAVE YOUR HEALTH.

And perhaps you don't have your health. Perhaps you are sick and then you definitely have a right to complain. Don't you?

I invite you to take a quick look at Stephen Hawking's profile (http://en.wikipedia.org/wiki/Stephen_Hawking). He is a world renowned physicist with ALS who is almost entirely paralyzed and communicates through a speech generating device, and yet he married twice and has three children and three grandchildren.

No matter what we have or don't currently have, we can always find blessings in our lives, in ourselves.

You may never have everything you want, but if you can stop, think and count your blessings, I'm sure you'll find that you'll always have more than you need. If you feel blessed in your life, you will feel confidence in what you do.

But to prove it to you, put a picture of the one thing you consider to be *your* favorite blessing in the space below, or take it one step further and put a bunch of your blessings there. It can be anyone—family member, friend, neighbor, movie star—anything, just so long as you feel blessed when you look at it. I think you'll agree it belongs here, in your YOUlogy.

INSERT

YOUR

BLESSINGS

HERE

There you go. Now you have living proof that you ARE blessed, and it's right here in print.

Have Faith

I don't talk about religion much because I believe that's a personal matter, but I find it hard to separate my faith in myself from my faith in a higher power. As I mentioned earlier, there was a time in my life when I took to reading two psalms every morning. It was my way of asking a higher power to help me, but it was also a way of asking for my own help. I took to own my faith, to practice and appreciate it, to give me the power I needed to begin believing in myself again.

My faith in a greater power (a friendly universe, if you will) gave me confidence in myself and I couldn't even begin to think about repairing my life if I didn't think I was worth it and didn't have the confidence to go about it with hope and determination. You have to believe you're worth the creation of a full, purposeful life or you'll simply sit back and let things happen to you. You can read all the self-help books you want, watch all the videos, listen to all the tapes, go to the seminars, and follow the steps but, at the end of the day, if you don't believe you're worth all the effort, none of it will "stick."

I had to have faith before I could rebuild myself, but once I did, the rebuilding came easier. Not easy, mind you, or even simple, but *easier*. If I can rebuild my life from scratch, with no money, no home, no wife and no prospects, imagine what you can do starting with "okay."

Take it from me, you're worth it. How do I know that when I've never even met you? I just know. I know because we're all born with a gift. Every one of us on this planet is born with a unique, sincere and authentic gift that belongs to him or her.

Maybe it's a gift you can share with the rest of the world, or just your world. Maybe it makes you special to millions of people, or just a handful. Maybe this gift is worth millions, thousands, or hundreds. It's *your* gift, and it makes you special—but only if you discover it, tap into it, own it, and live it every day.

We're all born with a purpose. I genuinely believe that. Furthermore, whether you believe it or not, for most of us on this planet, our purpose is not simply to make money. Don't let that be your only passion or purpose in this life.

If you make money because of your passion, that's great. Remember though that three of the greatest people to ever live did not experience wealth. I'm talking about Mother Teresa, Mahatma Gandhi, and Moses. However, each was born with a specific gift.

Even with those gifts, they all had challenges. None of them lived an easy life and few of us ever will. Those who tell you life is easy either haven't lived through a challenge yet or are simply lying to you.

Life is full of challenges, but those challenges become easier to handle when we know our worth and what's waiting for us on the other side of them. Frankly, pursuing your passion can introduce you to a whole new set of trials. Starting a new business isn't easy. Neither is going back to school, or learning to play the guitar, or joining a band, or opening a nursery, or molding raw clay into works of art.

All effort is a challenge, and since life takes effort, life is by definition a challenge. But when you know your gifts and your talents and your passion, what a beautiful challenge it can be.

Conclusion

Putting It All Together

*"If we did all the things we are capable of doing,
we would literally astound ourselves."*
**Thomas Edison (1847–1931), Inventor and salesman
who frequently worked more than forty hours straight**

A eulogy is typically reserved for endings. It's what we read at the end of someone's life to remind the living of what the recently deceased accomplished.

While thorough, and often impressive, it always feels...incomplete, doesn't it? No matter how long we live, there is always one more thing we'd like to have added to our eulogy. A skydiving trip or a luxury vacation. A zoom in a cherry-red racecar or another waltz with our spouse. Another walk with our dog, another award on the wall, another nice dinner, or another stroll on the beach at sunset.

But this book isn't about endings; it's about beginnings. It's about finding your passion and putting it to work for you and your family. It's about living your life and not "dying" it.

So even though we're at the end of our journey together, your journey is just beginning. It is my sincere hope that you've found inspiration, even preparation, in the preceding one hundred or so pages. I hope that you've found our time together worthwhile and that I've given you the tools you need not only to find your passion, but also to live it.

Now it is time to write and live your own YOUlogy. Now, while you're living, driving, breathing, and thriving. Don't be the way I was for so many years, dying my life rather than living it. Don't just exist, muddling through because you don't think you have the time, talent or treasure to pursue your true passion. Live your life.

Live every moment by doing what you love the most, not just tomorrow, but today. In the last few chapters, I introduced my concept of baby steps, of taking one step at a time. I'm not asking you to shut this book and completely, totally and permanently alter your existence.

What I am asking is that you do one thing, one small thing, to commit to making those changes I talked about, to following the path you've chosen for yourself, once and for all.

It can be anything.

- Google an opportunity you're interested in.
- Bookmark the contact page for that franchise you've always wanted to start.
- Order a catalog from the college program you want to get into.
- Check out a book from the library on pottery, nurseries, or whatever your passion is.
- Ask a mentor for advice.
- Talk about your passion with your spouse, partner, family, or friend.

Whatever it is, no matter how big or small, how mundane or game changing, just start. *Now*. Don't wait until tomorrow when the alarm clock goes off, life will just get in the way again. Don't wait until tonight when you get home from work, you'll be too tired. Do something right now to move your life toward your passion. Take a break, reward yourself and…Start. Something. Right. Now.

Remember, we're not promised anything in this life, so do something today that is going to help you live a better tomorrow. If you're stuck, or need advice or an idea, or just want to brag about what you did to start writing your YOUlogy today, I'd love to help out and/or hear about it. So visit me at www.RedInspires.com and drop me a line, or e-mail me directly at info@redinspires.com.

Remember, my passion is helping you find *your* passion and I'm never too busy to live my passion. Whether in person for your next speaking engagement, through my blogs or videos, or simply via e-mail or text, I can't wait to hear your YOUlogy!

But first, you'll have to write it. And this is where you'll start...

About the Author

Red Katz

R ed Katz is a dynamic, "real world" professional keynote speaker who has the unique ability to connect, motivate and inspire even the most buttoned-down of audiences in a matter of minutes.

Over the last twenty years, Red Katz has been able to leverage his natural speaking talent to find professional success as an entrepreneur. He has spent the last ten of those years cultivating his passion for motivating others through his active membership and leadership in the prestigious speaking organization, Toastmasters International, as well as The Mankind Project. As a result, he has been able to realize his dream by delivering powerful keynote speeches for a wide variety of corporate and social organizations.

If you have a team that needs to be reenergized, a group or organization facing a unique set of challenges, or a company that seems to be sinking into the abyss of "no," a few minutes with Red Katz is just the antidote.

In today's hard-to-navigate environment, it is more important than ever for individuals to find their inner "rock star" and pave their own path to success. Consider Red Katz your own personal guide to this transformation.

Red is available for keynote speeches at your conference or organization. Contact him at www.RedInspires.com and drop him a line or e-mail him directly at red@redinspires.com. He'd love to hear from you!

Recommended Readings

Bolles, Richard N. 2012. *What Color Is Your Parachute?* Berkeley, CA: Ten Speed Press.

Bronson, Po. 2006. *What Should I Do with My Life? The True Story of People Who Answered the Ultimate Question.* New York City: Ballantine Books.

Fulghum, Robert. 1986. *All I Really Needed to Know I Learned in Kindergarten.* New York City: Ballantine Books.

Made in the USA
Charleston, SC
20 December 2014